KILTS ACROSS
THE JORDAN

To
MY DEAD COMRADES
OF
THE LONDON SCOTTISH

"WIRE ROADS !"

Frontispiece.

KILTS ACROSS THE JORDAN

BEING EXPERIENCES AND IMPRESSIONS
WITH THE SECOND BATTALION
"LONDON SCOTTISH" IN PALESTINE

BY

BERNARD BLASER

(BATTALION SCOUT AND "MAPPER")

WITH A PREFACE BY

FIELD-MARSHAL VISCOUNT ALLENBY, G.C.B., G.C.M.G

PHOTOGRAPHS AND MAPS

Bernard Blaser

The Naval & Military Press Ltd

in association with

The National Army Museum, London

Published jointly by

The Naval & Military Press Ltd
Unit 10 Ridgewood Industrial Park,
Uckfield, East Sussex,
TN22 5QE England

Tel: +44 (0) 1825 749494
Fax: +44 (0) 1825 765701

www.naval-military-press.com
www.military-genealogy.com
www.militarymaproom.com

and

The National Army Museum, London
www.national-army-museum.ac.uk

Printed and bound in Great Britain by
CPI Antony Rowe, Chippenham and Eastbourne

*In reprinting in facsimile from the original, any imperfections are inevitably reproduced
and the quality may fall short of modern type and cartographic standards.*

PREFACE

I HAVE great pleasure in complying with the Author's request that I should write a few words as preface to this book.

The scenes described are, mostly, familiar to me; and I can affirm the accuracy of the narrative. I still possess some of the panoramic sketches, made by the Author, showing the Turkish positions before Jerusalem.

Palestine was occupied, and Jerusalem won, as the result of hard marching and fierce fighting, in which the Author of this book had a forward part. He tells us how war looks from the point of view of the man in the front row; and the record of his experiences makes fascinating reading.

He has made an important addition to the literature of the war, and his work will be greatly appreciated by all who assisted or are interested in that great adventure.

I recommend to everyone this book, written by one who was a member of that splendid fighting force which I had the honour to command, an Army wherein he and his companions in arms were second to none.

Allenby F. M.

CONTENTS

LIST OF ILLUSTRATIONS

PLATES

MAPS

CHAPTER I

His Majesty's Transport *Aragon*, steadily ploughing her way through the blue Mediterranean, was engaged upon the complicated operation of conveying her precious human cargo with care and precision through the Greek Archipelago, carefully avoiding too close proximity to those innumerable islands, and cautiously feeling her way through waters known to be liberally besprinkled with German submarines thirsting for blood. The weather, standardized to what we had been used to, was perfect. It was early morning, and as we gazed wonderingly across the stretch of deep blue, glassy water intervening, those little islands, with their sharp jagged cliffs appearing apparently from nowhere, were beautiful, veiled delicately in an opalescent gauze.

We were ordered to wear lifebelts and to keep our feet bare throughout the voyage, and this was religiously carried out, later to our discomfort, for as the sun rose higher, certain sections of the decks grew unbearably hot under his merciless rays. We had not exactly saloon accommodation, and at night every available inch of deck space, and every conceivable and inconceivable nook and cranny were occupied by the sleeping forms of men; but then, were we not on our way to the East, the mysterious, ever sunny East?

We were all filled with that feeling of expectancy

which normal mortals experience on approaching a strange land, but which is intensified tremendously in those of artistic temperament. Our tame rumour experts told us two years previously that we were destined for Egypt, but little then did they know of the truth of their prophecy, and none dreamt it would be by such a devious route as Vimy Ridge, Mount Olympus and Macedonia.

Except for putting into Mudros Harbour, an extensive natural refuge, to take off some unfortunate fellows who had been recently torpedoed, we had quite a pleasantly uneventful voyage.

We had been voyaging about a day, and had just cleared the Greek Archipelago, when we discerned with great interest a school of porpoises just a few yards ahead of the ship. It seemed they had assumed guardianship over us, for with unceasing persistency they piloted us through the water, plunging in graceful sweeping movements, crossing and recrossing our bows, occasionally darting to the right or left, presumably in quest of food, to return immediately to take up the responsibility for our safety, as though the two smart destroyers provided for the purpose were really of *no* consequence.

It was a radiant afternoon and the fourth day of the voyage. The blue dome above, unsullied by clouds, merged on all sides into the deep blue ocean. Far across the blue waters we first saw the coast of Egypt gleaming in the sun—a vague white streak on the horizon. As we drew nearer, so the far-off coast gradually came into focus, the whole landscape sorting itself out, gaps in the stretch of white proclaiming their identity as clusters of palms, and jumbled shadows and shapes forming themselves into buildings and villages.

While gazing, eager with anticipation, at the vivi-fying scene before us, a dark speck separated itself from the panorama and came in our direction. A closer view proved it to be a tug, and as it drew along-side, a companion-way was lowered, and several brightly robed beturbaned figures and divers dusky individuals in European costume—but for the native tarboosh—came aboard. With much swagger and show of self-esteem they made their way to the Com-mander's cabin, where they were received as personages of importance, being of the order of Customs and Excise.

Meanwhile, having been deserted by our fishy escort, the two destroyers steamed ahead and, finding all clear, sent signals to that effect, whereupon we made towards the harbour, which could be easily dis-tinguished by the huge lighthouse at the head of the breakwater.

After about an hour's skilful manœuvring we passed through the outer harbour, wherein was a wonderful conglomeration of shipping moored in picturesque confusion; native dhows and small coasting steamers, every bit as important in themselves as the palatial liners and warships of the latest type with which they were rubbing maritime shoulders, until at last we came to rest alongside an inner wharf, our good ship having completed one more, her penultimate, voyage,[1] and having introduced many curious and wondering souls to the glamour and mystery of the East.

Preparations for disembarkation were soon in full swing. Men crowded to the sides of the boat, craning their necks in their eagerness to see new sights. Ready-packed sets of equipment and rifles were heaped on the decks in places best calculated to trip

---

[1] H.M.T. *Aragon* was torpedoed during her next voyage.

up the unwary, and some men were busily packing gear and colossal quantities of property into the extremely diminutive capacity provided in their packs. Groups were gathered in a very limited space playing the inevitable last few rounds of cards, sitting upon other people's equipment, for which the owners were instituting a futile search; others were engaged in the popular pastime of dodging N.C.O.'s eager to form fatigue parties.

Numbers of happy-go-lucky individuals, who leave everything to the last minute, are never flurried, and will not be hurried, and those who were quite ready, either clustered together on the landward side endeavouring to catch a glimpse of the shore, or were leaning over the rail on the other side, buying fruit, nuts, and mysterious native concoctions from the " bum-boats," which were clamouring alongside in a veritable swarm, lowering the money in a basket at the end of a line to the rascally vendors below, and hauling up whatever they chose to give.   It was the curiosity of the troops alone that allowed such arbitrary business principles on the part of the natives.

Even the least imaginative traveller would experience a certain wondering curiosity upon arriving at an Eastern port, confronted as he is by new scenes and strange people rendered the more attractive by reason of tales and traditions of world-wide renown. As I was about to set foot on the land of this historic people I was all speculation as to what the modern Egyptian would be like.   I had seen Egyptian students in London dressed, of course, in European clothes, with spectacles and learned expression complete, and now on entering Egypt and seeing the same individuals at home, I had great difficulty in connecting the two, with the exception perhaps in the comparison of their colouring.

Finding myself in the midst of the muddle and confusion on deck, where the air resounded with shouts of laughter and rang with echoes of joviality of both European and Egyptian origin, I engineered a passage through the crowd, exercising much patience and a certain diplomacy, and eventually gained the rail on the landward side. Just below me was the stone wharf-side, in appearance just like any other wharf-side at home, along which were several sets of railway lines, while the usual unprepossessing storehouses and sheds formed the background. As we were to disembark at nine o'clock that evening and entrain straightway, shunting operations were in progress. The Battalion's baggage was being unloaded and deposited—or, to use the appropriate military expression, " dumped "—in huge piles at a spot convenient for loading on to the train, and in the midst of this scene a native brawl was in progress.

A number of nondescript, bedraggled creatures of all ages and sizes, clad in a rare assortment of ragged garments, for the most part dirty white, relieved here and there by blue and red, and whose feet were bare, were apparently engaged in carrying the luggage from the ship's side to the dump by the railway. One assumed from the gruffness of the voices now raised in a torrent of execration and abuse that these strange-looking individuals were of the male persuasion, for, indeed, that is the only means a stranger has of determining their sex. One of them, very tall, thin, and bent beneath a huge piece of baggage—undoubtedly a Subaltern's kit—suddenly meeting a short, squat, swarthy person, immediately threw down his load and entered into stormy altercation with him. They shouted at each other for some minutes, gesticulating violently, their baggage lying neglected upon the ground, the argument becoming hotter and hotter, each adopting a threatening attitude, as though about to fly at the other's throat, when they received a sudden interruption. A number of sharp whacks upon their respective bodies, delivered in quick succession with a thick stick by a short, thick-set British soldier on police duty, who had been standing quietly by, seemed to act as a sobering tonic. Without further ado and not stopping to ask questions, they instantly scrambled for their loads and went their respective ways. Many men who witnessed this incident ejaculated murmurs of protest, while others, more callous and hardened, laughed, thinking it great sport. My feelings were mixed, sympathy for the chastised intermingling with the dictates of experience in allowing our military friend with the thick stick to know his business best. We learned very soon afterwards, however, that this summary treatment is the only logic these natives understand, for in everyday dealings with them, to use a common metaphor, if you give them a yard they are presumptuous enough to help themselves immediately to the remaining 1,759.

Of course, it is a punishable offence on the part of a British soldier to strike a native—in the military penal code, for all practical purposes, the act of *being caught* constitutes the crime. Attached to all labouring gangs of natives is a huge fellow, ostensibly of higher caste, who acts as foreman, or " Rice " as he is called, and who carries a thick thong whip with which to administer justice amongst his mob. Upon any sign of laziness or disobedience he never fails to exercise full use of the privileges of his exalted position—a survival of the ancient system of employing task-masters. The labourer, upon being thus beaten, seldom shows fight, but slinks away like a whipped cur.

"So this is the modern Egyptian," thought I, contemplating the scene before me. Well, no doubt this rabble below on the wharf were of the lowest order, and one could hardly expect to find an educated Egyptian working as a dockside labourer. No doubt I should very soon have further opportunities of seeing the Egyptian at home, but in other surroundings and under different circumstances.

Nevertheless, I was disappointed, although, of course, I hardly expected to see the fine, dignified type of which we read, but I must say that my first impression on arrival, created by this dirty howling mob, dispelled my fanciful ideas of the present-day Egyptian.

CHAPTER II

WE had not been informed officially that we were bound for Egypt before we boarded the good ship we were just about to leave. A soldier's duty, first and last, is to do as he is told. Upon the order, " By the right—quick—*March!* " he simply steps off with his left foot and marches; he may be marching to Heaven or to Hell, but that is no concern of his. Moreover, it is not policy to publish the destination of a body of troops in time of war. We drew our own conclusions, however, that British territory was to be *our* destination when we were paid in British currency before leaving Salonica, and were advised to exchange our Greek money for British; but it was not until we had been a day or so at sea that we came to know we were bound for Alexandria.

Of course, the ever-present individual, who gleans private information from a " most reliable source," which he promptly imparts, in the strictest confidence, to everybody, had been at work as usual, but the rumour soon became strong enough hardly to need confirmation. A soldier's life is full of rumours. His very existence is composed of them. He has fresh ones served with every meal, and when he is unfortunate enough not to have a meal he extracts as much nourishment as possible from the last issue, and, adopting the Micawber attitude, hopes for the best. His accoutrement is not complete without that emergency supply of rumours which every soldier carries carefully stored away in his mind, wrapped in the scant covering of any flimsy tissue of fact which he may possess.

Alexandria! It was early evening; the sun was still shining on the housetops, harbour and shipping, bathing the whole scene in a warm yellow light, while interspersed between the buildings, and forming the background, could be seen palm trees, creating a pleasant relief to the eye and giving a decorative effect to the sun-baked buildings around.

I stood against the rail ruminating as the red orb of the sun disappeared below the Western horizon. Alexandria, founded by Alexander the Great 330 years B.C., is still a colossal trading centre, a mart for every kind of merchandise after over 2,000 years! How I wished that I might be free just to step off the boat and wander at will over the historic city—or even to peep into one of the main streets, when, maybe, I should catch a glimpse of the Egyptian of my fancies, the tall, dignified type, and so eradicate from my mind, until I had an opportunity of becoming familiar with the Egyptians as a people, the unfavourable impression created by the mob of scallawags on the wharf! But no, we were not out upon a sight-seeing expedition. There was work before us—a great object had yet to be accomplished. Realizing the futility of further dwelling upon the wonders of the place to which Fate had brought me, full of tradition and teeming with interest as I knew it to be, there was only one thing to do, and that at once to return to earth and attend to the material matters of the moment.

We duly disembarked at nine o'clock that night, and entrained immediately. The local and troop trains of the Egyptian State Railways are composed of long coaches arranged with seats to accommodate two, placed at right angles to the sides with a passage-way down the centre, a small platform at each end affording means of ingress and egress. Having disposed of our impedimenta in the coach as only troops know how, we settled down to spend as com-fortable a night as possible. There was no moon, though an occasional village situated amidst palms could be discerned silhouetted against the intense blue sky, which was studded with myriads of bright stars.

Very soon after the train started, conversation languished, heads began to nod, and those whose positions were conducive to sleep were soon in the land of dreams. It is remarkable how men can settle down under all conditions, and in any circumstances, when campaigning. Those who were fortunate enough to get places next the windows had support on two sides, and enjoyed comparative comfort; whilst those next the gangway either slept with their chins on their chests or with their heads resting on the shoulders of their near companions.

We had been warned before entraining to take particular care of our rifles and kit, but one man, heedless of this, placed his complete marching order equipment on the platform at the end of the coach, where, no doubt, he thought it would be as safe as anywhere else. His optimism, however, proved fatal. Amongst the lower-class natives, or " Gyppoes " as we soon learned to call them, kleptomania appears to be a chronic disease, which no amount of supervision can cure. The train had just passed through a village at a moderate speed when the aforementioned kit was found to be missing. A systematic search was made, resulting in nothing but the conclusion that a native had apparently boarded the train whilst in motion, and, overcome by an irresistible temptation, seized the entire equipment, and made off with it unseen into the night—probably an achievement coincident with the routine of his daily life. Later a Court of Inquiry was held on the subject of our friend's loss, and as a penalty for his carelessness he had to pay for the replacement of the missing articles of military property, in addition to suffering the loss of any personal effects of which he may have been possessed.

It was my happy lot to occupy a seat by an open window, through which the warm night air, laden with those subtle scents peculiar to the East, came stealing, soothing my fast-ebbing senses, wafting me away to other spheres, to the monotonous accompaniment of the rattling train, whose steady rhythm was disturbed ever and anon by a deep snore from one or other of my companions.

I must have been dozing for some time, when, like a blow across the head from an unknown hand, a discordant sound broke into the harmony of my slumbers. I roused myself with an effort, to become conscious of a hoarse voice bawling something quite unintelligible, and too close to my ear to be exactly pleasant. Starting up, I found that the train had stopped in a station, and that he of the voice responsible for rudely disturbing me was a white-robed, dark-visaged person, proclaiming to all and sundry that he had hard-boiled eggs for sale by bawling " Eggs-a-cook " in the carriage windows.

The station was Zag-a-zig, a large railway junction, and one of the official stopping-places during our journey, approximately two-thirds of the way to Ismalia, our destination.

By this time there was a general stir all round. Men like myself roused out of their sleep were stretching and yawning, and exchanging fragments of conversation, while many were buying eggs from the merchant in the robes, so I accepted the situation philosophically, and followed their example. The dusky-faced vendor was selling them at two for one piastre (2½d.), and was kind enough to accept British currency at the rate of exchange of four piastres to a shilling (thereby gaining 2d.). I bought four eggs, and handed him a shilling, which he promptly placed in his mouth as I waited for my change. He began to fumble amongst his draperies, first on one side, then on the other, burying his arm deeply amongst his robes until the search in these directions proving unsuccessful he decided to try other likely fields, and plunged his arm down his chest just as the train began to move slowly on. In spite of my ignorance of the little ways these merchants have in matters of business, I harboured within me a keen sense of distrust, so, without more ado, I reached out and grabbed four more eggs from his basket, thereby concluding the transaction, and sank back into my seat as the train gained speed, very satisfied that I had been smart enough to prevent this " Gyppo " from cheating me, as, I verily believe, was his intent.

The eggs were hard-boiled, and as tough as india-rubber. As we afterwards learned, they are cooked in Nature's oven, being left for some hours in the sun beneath a thin covering of sand. Oh, ye of weak digestion! forgive me if I disturb your equanimity by so outraging your gastronomic principles, but it is a fact that, hard as those hard-boiled eggs were, we lost no time in disposing of them just as they were (excepting the major portion of the shells, of course), without embellishment or accompaniment of any kind, and with much relish notwithstanding.

In addition to egg merchants, there were natives selling various commodities, including an attractive brand of champagne, in dark-coloured bottles bearing a well-known label, the corks of which were bound in the usual way. Several men at the other end of the carriage combined, and procured a bottle of this excellent sparkling wine for 25 piastres (4s. 6d.), and as the train proceeded on its journey prepared thoroughly to enjoy their supper of cakes, buns and hard-boiled eggs, now augmented and glorified by the newly acquired luxury. Each would-be participant, eager with excitement, busied himself in preparation for the feast, face aglow with wide-eyed expectancy, watching the operation of opening the bottle. Twelve months' enforced denial from the good things of the earth enhances the qualities of champagne indeed. The cork was carefully removed, and mugs were passed along. By the dim light from the carriage lamp the Master of Ceremonies poured some of the precious liquor into each, but at the first sip an instantaneous change passed over the group. The cherished hopes of those thirsty warriors were immediately dashed to the ground (and beyond) upon tasting the contents of that dearly purchased bottle, which turned out to be nothing stronger than WATER—and none of the purest at that.

I need not record the shower of maledictions heaped

upon the head of that rascally " Gyppo," but it will suffice to say that this swindle helped to fan into flame the fire of distrust and suspicion which was fast kindling in the hearts of us all.

Very soon everybody settled down again, and all was quiet, save for the monotonous rattle of the train.

CHAPTER III

AT ISMALIA (*July*, 1917)

At dawn next morning we reached our destination, the journey having occupied about eight hours. We detrained at a special military siding close to a veritable maze of tents affording accommodation for many thousands of troops.

In the one direction, where the view was not composed of lines upon lines of tents, vast stretches of sand met the eye, falling away to the horizon in gentle undulations, impressing the observer forcibly with the immensity and desolation of those great sandy wastes which comprise the major portion of Northern Africa. In the other direction, about two miles away, groups of palm trees relieved the monotony of the sand, houses peeped out amid the foliage, the whole scene being dominated by a majestic minaret rearing its grace and beauty high above all its surroundings. This was Ismalia, the beauty spot of the Suez.

After the usual bustle of detraining, the Battalion formed up in "column of route," and marched a short distance to an empty camp, where we were allotted tents in which we duly installed ourselves. It was a great pleasure to find that tea was awaiting us, made by another Battalion in the Brigade which had arrived the day before, and after partaking of refreshment we settled down to rest after our journey. Following the cramped accommodation of the Transport and the night journey in the train, we found no difficulty whatever in sleeping through the remainder of the day, stretched on the soft sand in those shady tents.

Although we had experienced fairly hot weather in that malaria-infested region, Macedonia, it was necessary that we should become acclimatized to the new conditions we were to meet, which accounted for our stay of about three weeks at Ismalia. During this time we were put through two hours' training morning and evening, thus escaping the midday heat.

It was now that the rumour-mongers were again presented with a favourable opportunity for exerting their powers of prophecy, of which they availed themselves whole-heartedly. Some had it that, as we had not had a "rest" for twelve months, we were going to Cairo on garrison duty; others were convinced that Khartoum was to be the scene of our inactivities, while those incorrigible pessimists, who, however, often turn out to be substantially correct, said that we were undoubtedly under orders to move straight "up the line" to take part in a "great offensive." We had hitherto been too absorbed in our own particular sections of line on the two European fronts to have gleaned much information about this one. In fact our acquaintance with it was so slight that few even knew where it was situated, except in a general sense of direction, so this latter piece of information produced little effect. However, it has been my experience whilst campaigning that, of a number of conflicting rumours, it is safest, if not to believe, at least to place more faith in those which act most directly contrary to one's own wishes.

After a few days we commenced training in earnest,

practising that wretched " open attack " time and time again over some neighbouring sandhills, until we practically knew every inch of the ground. The whole scheme operated like clockwork and those much ill used sandhills fairly shrank before our thirsty onslaughts.

We also practised making bivouacs with our blankets and rifles, with the aid of wooden pegs and sundry pieces of string, twine or rope which we managed to gather together. This was quite simply done by first tying two blankets together at the two corresponding corners of each, standing two rifles (with sheathed bayonets fixed) upright one blanket length apart, and fastening with more pieces of string the two joints of the blankets on to the tops of the respective rifles. More string connected the rifle tops with pegs driven into the ground in line with the join, and more pegs fixed the four outside corners of the blankets in their proper positions. This simple structure made quite an effective shelter from the heat of the sun by day, and the heavy dews by night, always providing, of course, that the weather conditions were favourable, for, indeed, it needed but a slight wind to overstrain those brave little pegs which were doing their utmost to maintain their position in the loose sand, and upon whose failure the whole wonderful structure would collapse.

Well, it is not necessary to practise the "attack" feverishly to do garrison duty, nor would we need blanket bivouacs within the sheltered precincts of a garrison station, both of which facts completely exploded the theories of those kind friends who had consigned us to so congenial an occupation—much to their disgust. In the face of these preparations, therefore, it became amply manifest that we were destined for " up the line," to take part in whatever operations the powers-that-be had kindly thought out for us.

It must not be imagined, however, that our short stay at Ismalia was without its pleasures and attractions. Bathing parties were arranged, and those who so desired marched about a mile and a half across the sand (a very laborious pastime, about which there is more to say later) to Lake Timsâh (the Crocodile Lake), a large sheet of salt water, through which passes the Suez Canal. I say salt water advisedly, for indeed it was like brine—in fact it *was* brine, and though the facilities for swimming were very appreciable, they could not be indulged in without a considerable measure of discomfort in the shape of parched throats, sore nasal passages and smarting eyes.

One day fatigue parties came struggling into the camp groaning beneath the weight of huge bales, the contents of which proved to be khaki drill slacks. We spent nearly the whole of the next morning being fitted, or rather misfitted, with them, and in the afternoon, just as everybody was busy cutting and sewing to make them correspond more or less to individual frames and tastes, the slacks were called in. As we were a kilted regiment and already had knee shorts, this latter action was the more easily understood. It was very amusing, however, to see fellows running about with kilts on over their slacks, which in many instances were so long that no portion of their boots could be seen. After all, maybe, it was the object of the authorities to amuse us and create a little diversion. If so, they succeeded beyond all expectations, though perhaps at a greater expense than they calculated.

Naturally the town of Ismalia was the chief attraction, and the authorities very graciously issued an order that a certain percentage of each Unit would be allowed to visit the town on pass every day after 2 p.m. This order, though, did not prevent the major portion of the Battalion from enjoying the delights of Ismalia to the full, for I know of very few who stayed in camp for the want of a pass.

Ismalia, named after the successor of Sa'id Pasha, the ex-Khedive, is the most modern of the three towns that have sprung up upon the advent of De Lesseps' great masterpiece. It is situated at the angle where the railway and the Freshwater Canal change the northerly course they pursue from Suez, and strike off in a westerly direction across the " Land of Goshen " to Zag-a-zig, where again they change direction, following a southerly course to Cairo. In recent years a new line of railway has been constructed from Port Said, running parallel with the Canal for some distance, and effecting a junction at Ismalia with the line from Suez.

The pedestrian on his way to the town, after leaving Moaska, where our camp was situated, proceeds along a fairly good road parallel with the Freshwater Canal. This canal is very ancient indeed, existing before the Israelites' captivity in Egypt, when it undoubtedly formed an important link between the traders of the East and the merchants of Memphis. It is frequently called the " Sweetwater Canal," that presumably being an alternative name to distinguish it from the great salt-water canal which has in later years come into being. This latter name, however, most certainly belies it, for although I have never tasted it—and do not know anyone who has— it is very thick and muddy in appearance, and

altogether quite unappetizing. Traffic in the shape
of picturesque native dhows with peculiar turned-up
bows and huge lateen sails are still to be seen passing
up and down this canal, carrying all kinds of
merchandise just as they did in the ancient days, when
it was one of the main trade routes of the then known
world.

The native quarter, which is that first encountered,
lies to the left of the road and forms the centre of
interest of this very Europeanized town. The
outstanding feature is the Mosque with its tall minaret,
just a little back from the road, and is naturally an
object of much curiosity and interest to the newcomer.
The streets are for the most part narrow and none too
clean. Passing down the centre of the road (for
nobody dreams of using the pavements except the
shopkeepers, who make full use of them to display
their wares), one's nostrils are assailed by those not
unpleasant odours emanating from the shops and
warehouses of all Eastern market-places. The shops
are quite attractive, and there is a number of small
one-roomed establishments which the owners are
presumptuous enough to call bazaars. These are
generally kept by natives or Greeks, who are really
very enterprising. We had been at Ismalia barely
a couple of days when they were selling table
centres embroidered with the various regimental
crests.

Silk goods and metal articles worked in Egyptian
designs seemed to predominate. There were also
dozens of other knick-knacks to be sold, some genuine
and some cheap-looking imitations, and it was difficult
to tell the difference. The art of discriminating
between the two, of course, comes with experience—
sometimes dearly purchased.

After a very entertaining, though perhaps expensive, hour's sojourn in one of these bazaars you would saunter down the street somewhat dazed, wondering whether sundry relatives and dear friends would really ever get the attractive little presents which, at the cost of much thought and patience and many piastres, you had selected for their pleasure.

Then there were the restaurants, which were generally kept by Greeks, who possessed the valuable asset of knowing how to cater for hungry troops longing for a change from Army fare—and they profited considerably thereby. Fish there was in abundance (though I could never tell what particular kind), and fried eggs by the dozen, which, with many other accompaniments, provided a very palatable and satisfying repast. A visit to Ismalia was not complete without having a meal at one of these restaurants, in fact that was one of the chief items.

Upon returning to camp at night great excitement would ensue when fellows related their experiences, compared notes, and generally criticized each other's acquisitions from the bazaars, volunteering not too flattering opinions upon one's business capabilities and advice for future guidance.

CHAPTER IV

FROM ISMALIA, ACROSS SINAI TO BELAH (*July,* 1917)

THE time for our departure from Ismalia came only too soon. Preparations were made for a three days' trek. Goods and chattels were gathered together, equipments packed, and at the appointed time one evening, the Battalion formed up and marched through the town, our actual ultimate destination remaining as obscure as ever.

As we passed along the smooth, tarred macadam roads, shaded by large overhanging trees, numbers of the population, both European and native, stood by the wayside watching us, actuated by that curiosity always excited by troops marching to the skirl of pipes and the beat of drums.

Upon our approach native men and women, with swarms of children, came running from the side streets and by-ways to see the soldiers pass. The soldiers were grim and uninterested, and perspired profusely under the fierce rays of Old Sol, who, as though cognizant of the fact that the day was fast closing in, seemed to utilize the remaining few hours in pouring forth enough of his radiant heat upon us poor mortals, struggling beneath the weight we carried, to last us through the chilly night till he greeted us again over the Eastern horizon.

After passing through a thick clump of palm

trees we emerged on to the open road and saw sand, nothing but sand on every side, our sole medium to inspiration, and our only means of mental relief from the discomforts of our heavy loads.

The Company cookers, facetiously termed "Artillery" by Infantrymen, were belching forth volumes of smoke *en route*, thereby informing us that they were boiling water, ready for making tea as soon as we should arrive at the camping-ground.

About an hour after dusk, having marched some eight miles, we reached El Ferdan, one of the many Canal stations. Here we turned off to the left of the road, and encamped on the sand for the night.

It was the practice of many of the younger and more inexperienced of our number upon arrival in camp, having surreptitiously consumed all the water in their bottles during the march, to rush off immediately to any likely spot in search of drinking water. Here, alongside the Canal, a water pipe had been laid, and at each station, and any intermediate spot used for camping, a system of water taps was fixed, being fed by the pipe. It did not take our young friends very long to scent these out, and before we had been in camp many minutes half the Battalion had crossed the few hundred yards and were swarming round those water taps like ants, some with water-bottles to replenish and some without, but all with first-class thirsts. The more experienced warriors, however, saved water in their bottles sufficient for their immediate needs, and lighting pipes or cigarettes, sat about in groups waiting until our worthy cooks had made the precious tea.

At last it was ready, and one pint of that steaming strong brown fluid would be issued to every man. I have known many men in civilian life who

C

seldom drank tea. Now they swear by it as a most refreshing beverage and valuable stimulant. I am one of them. It is necessary in order to appreciate tea fully to have marched beneath a scorching sun, your back aching to breaking-point under the weight of your pack, feet burning and painful, your tongue feeling too large for your mouth, and every drop of moisture appearing to have left your creaking body. Upon the completion of the last stage of the march, you arrive at the camping-ground in this deplorable condition, fling off your equipment, and, heedless of the state of the ground, lie full length and gasp. It is then, if arrangements have been properly regulated (though it is not often possible), that after a few minutes' rest the welcome tea is ready. Having partaken of your share, and having probably burnt your tongue in your eagerness, you feel an entirely different creature from the old crock who struggled into camp a little while ago.

After disposing of the remaining portion of the day's rations (if any) to the accompaniment of the indispensable tea (each man carried his own dry rations, such as bread or biscuits, jam, dried fruit, and bully beef), everybody settled down for the night, or, to use a simple military colloquialism, "creased up." Few, if any, erected bivouacs. Practically all preferred to sleep in the open, wrapped in a blanket, rather than waste time in putting a bivouac together, and so sacrifice the warmth of a covering.

It was a simple matter to lay one's bed and occupy it. Having extracted the blanket from the pack and spread it out on the sand, arranged the pack at one end as a pillow and laid oneself down on one-half of the blanket, using the other half as a covering, the operation was completed. It is always advisable to remove from the "pillow" all spare tins of bully beef and other articles of a like degree of hardness and shape, whose pointed corners are given to investigating the intricacies of the ear and are therefore hardly conducive to peaceful slumber. Such an oversight as this has often been responsible for a night of broken rest. Having successfully tucked and rolled oneself in bed (in the absence of a kindly sergeant-major to perform that office for you), a slight wriggle this way and that so displaces the sand as to form a kind of mould for the body. This stage being reached, which in the circumstances seems the acme of comfort, one lies there blinking up at the countless stars overhead until gradually carried away by Morpheus again to visit Ismalia maybe, and there buy up the contents of whole streets of bazaars, carrying the purchases in a colossal pack over hundreds of miles of desert.

Soon after dawn the next morning réveillé was sounded, and in a few minutes the whole camp was astir. The day was generally commenced with half an hour's physical drill—for we got so little exercise when on trek! Breakfast followed, after which we marched down to the Canal to bathe.

Throughout my fairly wide swimming experience, never have I enjoyed such glorious conditions as those prevailing during that short trek along the Suez Canal. The mornings were brilliant, the sun increasing in warmth as the hours stole on. The water of the Canal was a delicate emerald green, wonderfully clear and just a little salt, creating a pleasant contrast to the brine of Lake Timsâh. When in an upright position one's toes could be easily distinguished. We were indeed very grateful to be able to frolic about in this delightful water, especially so after our hot march of the previous evening.

Returning to camp, bivouacs were erected, beneath which we rested during the hottest hours of the day, either reading, or, if permitted by pestilential flies, sleeping.

Towards sunset the camp was struck, equipments packed, and we proceeded on another stage of our journey. It seemed very ironical that on the one side was the Canal, and on the other the railway— two excellent mediums of transit, and as we trudged somewhat resentfully along the road in between, empty motor-lorries continually passed and repassed us, seeming to grin at us in our misfortune, smothering us with dust in an endeavour to clog up our breathing apparatus and so impede what poor progress we *were* making.

On the second day of this trek we camped at another oasis along the Canal where a station is established. These stations consist of a large house, occupied by an official of the Canal authority, and around the house is generally a number of native huts and shanties. In this case, the house, with the small railway-station buildings, comprised all that went by the name of Tel el Balah. The routine was the same as on the previous night, followed in the morning by another enjoyable swim.

The third stage of our march brought us to Kantara, which, from a shabby mosque and a dozen or so native dwellings, had developed into a colossal canvas city and the largest military base in Egypt. Passing over the wooden bridge which spans the Canal opposite the railway station, we marched along a broad macadam road, lined on the right to a considerable depth with large camps. Everywhere there was canvas; remount depots, " details " camps, hospitals, Y.M.C.A. marquees, " Church Army" marquees, and numerous canteens and stores.   On the left of the road, behind barbed-wire fences, were the extensive store yards of the Ordnance Department, accommodating every conceivable kind of military supplies, from tent pegs to traction engines. Behind these again was the military railway station with adjoining goods yards, engine houses, repair shops, sidings of spare rolling-stock representing most of the chief railways of Great Britain, electric power-houses, and all the other component parts necessary for the construction of the gigantic military machine which was there established.

We marched on past those inviting camps, past the hospitable-looking Y.M.C.A. marquees and canteens, until we were quite clear of the suburbs of this immense canvas city, and eventually turned on to the sand and halted.   There we pitched camp.

Round about were old disused trenches dug in the sand and still protected by tangled masses of barbed wire.   These were reminiscent of the days of 1915, when the Turks, having crossed the Sinai Desert, attempted to cross the Suez Canal and so invade Egypt.   At that time the British Force was installed on the western side of the Canal, and the Turks on several occasions almost succeeded in effecting a crossing.   But for the timely arrival of a certain great British soldier it is difficult to say what turn events might have taken, perhaps altering the whole history of the Egyptian campaign.   This great soldier, however, immediately inquired whether the British force was protecting the Canal or the

Canal protecting it, supplying the answer himself by ordering the Canal to be crossed. This was done and a position taken up, about a mile from the eastern bank, in the system of trenches just referred to.

A story circulated in Kantara (which I am unable to confirm) that there is a rude memorial erected somewhere at Kantara East in memory of some British soldiers who lost their lives in a fight amongst themselves for possession of the very limited water-supply. The water was naturally heavily guarded, but men driven to extreme measures by thirst soon lose control of themselves, often with the result, as in this instance, of an awful calamity.

The maintenance of an efficient and adequate water-supply during operations in a desert country is vital to the success of the undertaking, and is generally attended by the greatest of difficulties. During that noble advance in 1915 under General Murray, when the comparatively small body of Infantry and Cavalry drove the Turks back across the Sinai Desert, a railway was laid, following in the wake of the advance at record speed—something like a mile a day—and water was carried to the troops by means of whole trainloads of tanks filled with the precious commodity. At the same time a huge pipe was laid alongside the railway over the whole of the distance, so that when the positions were consolidated before Gaza a good supply was assured, that through the pipe being augmented as and when required by water trains.

At dusk the following evening we struck camp once more, packed up our belongings, and marched to the station at Kantara East, where we waited for about two hours until the R.T.O., having by then finished his sumptuous meal and smoked his post-prandial cigar, condescended to find cattle-truck accommodation for one train-load of warriors.

I say cattle-trucks, but perhaps that is hardly just, for our trucks were clean, had roofs to them and open-work boarded sides, which was apparently deemed a sufficient reason for crowding in a few more soldiers.

Once duly entrained, we gave a phlegmatic jolt, and began to move. I think that was the most uncomfortable journey I have ever experienced, even outdoing in that respect a journey lasting nine days, from Taranto to Cherbourg, with thirty men and their kit to share the accommodation of one truck. It was a blessing that this journey lasted but twelve hours. We looked as though we had all been thrown headlong into the truck with our rifles and equipment, like so much luggage, and had remained in the positions we found ourselves in upon coming into contact with the floor. We were one jumbled mass of arms and legs, equipment, rifles and pith helmets. It was out of the question to lie down, and as the train bumped and jolted we gradually settled amongst our surroundings, being so wedged in and entangled with other people and their belongings that it was almost impossible to move. Occasionally a brave fellow, unable to endure his cramped position any longer, would attempt to extricate one of his numbed limbs, and searching about in the dark for some other place to put it, would alight upon another fellow's face, or some other vulnerable part, and would be at once exhorted to keep still on pain of an immediate introduction to blue fire and murder. And the train rattled on, so thoroughly shaking us all up that even the most seasoned campaigner found the greatest difficulty in sleeping.

I had been dozing for a little while, and was roused by the continued rush of cool night air against my face to find that we were in what appeared to be the heart of a desert. There was absolutely nothing to be seen on either side but vast stretches of barren sand, clothed in that dim bluish light so typical of Eastern nights, whilst above, the Heavens were studded with bright stars that seemed to hang like countless blue lamps.

At other times we were running close to the seashore, and by the light of the stars the Mediterranean could be distinctly seen lazily lapping on the beach. By dissociating myself from the noisy, roaring train, and contemplating the scene in imaginary solitude, the beauties of the mysterious light and the loneliness of it all were indeed very impressive.

The night wore on, and by dawn we passed through several thick clumps of palm trees. These became more frequent, until, approaching a small colony of engine sheds, workshops and sidings, the train came to a standstill at El Arish. There was a very large hospital here, together with rest-camps and Y.M.C.A. marquees, as at Kantara, though on a much smaller scale.

We were informed that a stop of an hour and a half was intended, and we immediately extricated ourselves from the tangle we had been in all night, and were very glad of the opportunity of stretching our cramped limbs.

The majority of fellows straightway besieged the canteen, which catered specially for troops travelling by rail, but several others and I made a bee-line for the sea, armed with towels and much eagerness. It took but a minute for us to undress and rush amid the breakers that were gently rolling in to the shore. The water was delightful, and frolicking about in the warm sun seemed a fair recompense for the extremely uncomfortable journey during the night.

The village of El Arish is situated about two miles from the coast, and had the appearance of a collection of white, flat-roofed buildings, from among which rose the inevitable minaret. The village, which was, of course, strictly out of bounds to the troops, stands close to the Wady El Arish. This Wady has its source in the "Wilderness of the Wanderings" in Central Sinai, and is identified as "The River of Egypt" mentioned in the Old Testament.

At the expiration of the time allocated for the halt everybody got aboard the train again, and we proceeded on our journey. After passing through some extensive clumps of shady palms, amidst some of which native huts were dotted about, the railway plunged into the barren desert. Sandhills were scattered about here and there, covered in places with patches of dried-up looking grass, and occasionally a stunted tree adorned the landscape in its struggle for an existence in that arid waste.

Running alongside the railway was a continuous ridge of sand, rising to a height of about three feet, obviously artificial, and strengthened or protected by stretches of "revetting." This, we afterwards learned, covered the water-pipe previously referred to.

At about ten o'clock we reached Dier el Belah, where a station had been established by the erection of several marquees and tents and the stacking of large quantities of stores.

Dier el Belah is one of many oases situated along this part of the coast from El Arish to Gaza, and is about five miles east of Khan Yunus. It was in this district that Napoleon, when returning to Egypt after his unsuccessful attempt to conquer Palestine, became so short of supplies that his troops were reduced to eating the bark of trees, and any other vegetation at all possible for human consumption. Fearing a mutiny, and the attendant consequences to himself to which such a contingency would give rise, he committed the very un-Napoleonic act of surreptitiously hurrying back to Alexandria, and returning to France in a small sailing boat, leaving his army to shift for itself.

Here we detrained, and at the invitation of the local branch of the Y.M.C.A. each man partook of a mug of cocoa and a piece of cake of substantial proportions; an item small enough in itself, but one which, in the circumstances, was greatly appreciated.

To reach our camping ground, which was situated by the sea, we had to traverse about two miles of sandhills. The surface sand was very loose and heavy, and this, combined with the midday heat, made the going extremely trying. However, all bad things, as well as good, come to an end, and it was not long before we had settled down and made ourselves comfortable. A stranger arriving a couple of hours afterwards would have thought we had been established there for weeks.

Our camp at Belah was situated on the sand-cliffs, which rose about thirty feet above the foreshore below. Bathing parades morning and evening were the order of the day, when the whole Battalion would be in the water at once. Several cliques were formed, which waged an aquatic war against each other, the supreme sacrifice being made when one of the "enemy," approaching you from the rear or from below the surface, succeeded in giving you a severe ducking. Opportunities would be sought to pay off old scores, and as all entered into the spirit of the game many were the exciting encounters that took place among the breakers.

During our stay here of about eight days the Battalion's turn came round for Divisional duties. These were not numerous, as the Division was really staying here *en route* for the "line." I was one of a dozen who were detailed for guard at a prisoners-of-war compound near the railway. The evening previously we attended the usual bathing parade. With the best of intentions a companion and I came out of the water early, and hurried back to camp in order to clean our equipment before the light failed. We were to be ready by three-thirty the next morning, so there would be no opportunity for doing so then. Our motive, however, was entirely incomprehensible to the military mind, and we were each "awarded" two days' "C.B." for our thoughtfulness.

The prisoners we guarded were accommodated in the usual barbed wire cages, and no shelter from the sun whatever was provided. The poor wretches hung pieces of rag and sacking up on the wire to create a small patch of shade in which to lay their heads. They were a very mixed crowd. The Turkish cavalry were kept separate from the infantry, being considered as of a much superior class. Deserters again were kept apart from those captured in engagements. In another cage, away from the Turks, were a number of Bedouins. They were a fierce-looking lot, though the features of some were decidedly handsome and very dignified. They had either been caught whilst acting as spies for the Turks, or were found under suspicious circumstances among our camps. One old fellow was a priest, and at intervals he produced a small copy of the Koran from the mysterious folds of his robes, and read out passages to the recumbent figures around. I do not know whether his companions derived much benefit from his reading, but it did not appear to impress them very much, for they remained in a state of absolute unconcern, and might have been asleep, until perhaps one of the sentries would have occasion to enter the enclosure, when they would immediately start up and be all on the alert.

A tent was erected in another enclosure, which housed a ragged old woman with a very small baby, which had a voice out of all proportion to its size. Through the whole night long the baby kept up a sort of oratorio on its own, which I am sure must have disturbed the gentry occupying the adjoining apartments. It was certainly a source of annoyance to the sentries during their turn of rest more than twice the distance away. I think the old woman must have been rather weary of the child too, for the next morning she offered it to one of the guard for five piastres, but as it would have taken up rather too much of the valuable space in his pack, and turned up its young nose at a bully beef diet, he declined the offer.

On a certain Sunday whilst we were at Belah a voluntary Church Parade was arranged for the evening. At the request of the Padre "any dress" was permitted. We had just been bathing, and the

majority were attired in shirts and drill shorts only.
In the absence of the onerous dress regulations of
tunics, belts and polished buttons, the attendance
was abnormal for a voluntary service, which clearly
went to show that the main objection is not to
the Church Parade, but to the fussy preparation
usually entailed.

Our good Padre had every reason to be gratified
at the response to his call, and I am certain that
a religious service could not have been more
impressive. Imagine five hundred healthy-looking
men sitting on the sand in a huge semi-circle,
reclining in various attitudes, their faces, arms and
legs bronzed by the sun, all listening intently to a
tall, athletic figure, standing with his back to the sea,
silhouetted against the horizon, where the glorious
vermilion of the setting sun merged into the blue
waters of the Mediterranean. What a contrast to
the artificialities of some of our present-day churches!
Here, in Christ's Church, the open air, the Gospel
was being preached in the very seat of its origin, and
the simple ceremony then taking place represented
just such a scene as when Christ preached to the
people amid similar surroundings. But for the
military costumes, and the bursting of shells away
to the north-east at Gaza, the aspect was one of
absolute peace.

CHAPTER V

THE DESERT

THE Desert, as applied to the vast sandy wastes in which we now found ourselves, is not without its beauties and attractions. Viewed under certain conditions and in certain circumstances, it is capable of presenting to the appreciative eye a splendour with which it is very difficult to find a parallel. Few would fail to be impressed by the intense solitude of the Desert at sunset when the sand, so white and dazzling during the daytime, gradually assumes a deep ochre, faintly tinted by the reflected vermilion of the sun as it rapidly, almost perceptibly, dips below the horizon. The author of " Eothen " says of the Desert :

" The earth is so samely that your eyes turn towards Heaven. You look to the sun, for he is your task-master, and by him you know the measure of the work that remains for you to do. He comes when you strike your tent in the early morning, and then for the first hour of the day . . . he stands at your near side and makes you know that the whole day's toil is before you; then for a while, and a long while, you see him no more, for you are veiled and shrouded and dare not look upon the greatness of his glory, but you know where he strides overhead by the touch of his flaming sword ; . . . but conquering time marches on, and by and by the descending sun has compassed the

Heaven and now softly touches your right arm, and throws your lank shadow over the sand right along the way for Persia."

How fascinating are the legends and mysteries of the Desert, and how easy it is to conjure up wonderful romances with such magnificent solitude stretched out before you, harbouring as it must do innumerable secrets of love and adventure, of hardship and death, never to be divulged!

The very bones that lie about bleached white by the sun fill the air with tragic mystery, and suggest all sorts of untold tales of privation and suffering; here the scattered frame of some unfortunate human being and there, protruding from the wind-swept sands, the remains of his faithful beast. Who it was who met such a fate and in what circumstances will never be known; but there lies the evidence smooth and white, nameless and unidentified, and there it will remain until swallowed up by the elements that caused its destruction.

We were about to make the acquaintance of the Desert. It would be our home for an unknown length of time to come. All its different aspects and characteristics, its beauty and relentless cruelty were soon to become familiar to us. No picturesque caravans would adorn the setting; we would see no more figures wrapped in coloured robes seated upon camels that lazily and mechanically shamble, one after the other, across the sand, but the grim, hard realities of warfare with all its attendant horrors and fluctuating fortunes would reign supreme.

CHAPTER VI

THE task of a Desert column had been allotted to us, and we were to be stationed at the extreme right of the line. We were to leave Dier el Belah and march to Sheikh Nuran. What Sheikh Nuran was and where, we knew not, except that it was a spot twelve miles inland, and owing to the absence of water *en route* the distance had to be accomplished across the sand in one stage. Accordingly, our camp was broken up one afternoon and the Brigade concentrated in a large oasis of palms enclosed by hedges of cactus.

In this oasis was an ancient stone well, dating back to the year A.D. 920 from which we filled our bottles with delicious water. Men of various other regiments were on duty regulating the water supply, and in conversation with them we learned that although we had a long march ahead of us, we should have the advantage of using a wire road for the greater part of the distance. This information, received quite credulously and in the good faith in which it was believed to have been given, cheered our hearts considerably. Twelve miles over good hard roads is one thing, but the same distance over loose sand is another.

We had seen examples of wire roads laid by the engineers. They were constructed by laying camel manure upon the sand when procurable, and on

48

top of that foundation ordinary wire netting was drawn tight and firmly pegged down. These roads are excellent to walk upon, giving considerable elasticity to the tread. Their use was strictly confined to pedestrian and light motor traffic, for it would have been most ill-advised to have the wire netting torn up by horses' hoofs, and of course camels are naturally adapted for walking on sand.

In due course the Brigade set out, our Battalion marching towards the rear of the column. We crossed the railway and continued over a low ridge, the surface under foot being composed of loose, fine dust. It was not even respectable sand, but a low-down, dirty-grey powder which, upon being disturbed, rose in clouds.

Before very long the head of the column was lost as in a mist. This was not very encouraging, but thoughts of the wire road kept up our spirits, and every fresh ridge and the intermediate hollows in that rolling expanse were eagerly dealt a searching glance for the object of our expectations. But still it failed to materialize. On we tramped, perspiring freely, the dust that rose about us clinging to our moist faces and bare knees until we presented a most humorous spectacle.

The humour of it, though, made an early exit from the piece. Our packs soon dominated what cheerful spirits we had left, and we could but settle down to our task with grim determination. After the regulation fifty minutes of marching, or rather slouching (it is impossible to march correctly in sand or dust), the leading companies came to attention from the " march at ease " (the oppressive preliminary to a halt), the order travelled along the length of the column, and in two minutes, upon the welcome sign being given, we halted. The relief felt at this juncture must be experienced to be realized, but it will suffice to say that to fall out to the side of the track, fling off equipment (carefully laying rifles thereon) and lie full length on the ground occupied but the fraction of a minute.   There were only ten precious minutes in which to rest, and we were to make the utmost of them.

At length a commotion is heard, the order given, whereupon you rise, harness yourself, and again take up your position in the ranks ready, more or less, to devour the remaining miles of the journey.

The experts have decided after much experience —probably other people's—that a rest of ten minutes in every hour is quite sufficient to allow for recuperation, and though at the time one feels it to be far too short, yet they are proved correct, for an extra five minutes would be just long enough for the muscles to become set and consequently, upon resuming, the joints would be stiff and movements awkward.

During the third hour the dust cloud that enveloped the whole brigade and hung about like a dense fog-bank became so serious a matter, that a halt of half an hour was ordered—a very unusual occurrence. We lay about, hot, tired and irritable, our faces covered with a thick coating of mud; but in spite of our extremely uncomfortable condition we could not refrain from laughing at each other's second-hand and very dilapidated appearance.   Those unfortunate people who habitually breathe through the mouth must have had a very bad time indeed.

Permission was given us to rinse out our mouths with water, but none was to be drunk.   Any man caught in the act of making a ferocious onslaught on his bottle could feel quite assured that fourteen days of the best Field Punishment would be the price to be

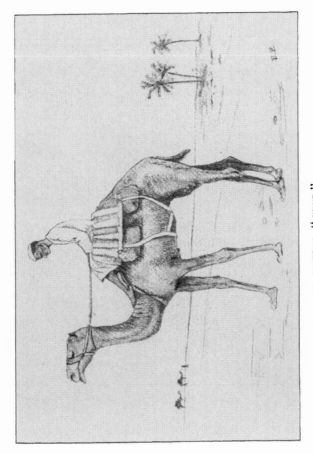

AN EASTERN "KNUT."

paid for his unlawful though undoubtedly much-needed drink.

My friend B——, an actor used to the good things of this life, was as thankful as I to sit down like any tramp by the roadside, and eat scraps of bread and jam, which comprised the " unexpended portion of the day's ration." Oh, how sweet were those few minutes of glorious inactivity, and how we dreaded the time when again the agonies of the march would sear our overburdened bodies. For the remainder of the halt we lay there using our packs as head-rests, and fearing even the exertion of conversation, intimated one to the other by nods and glances our unuttered appreciation of the respite we were thus enabled to enjoy.

At length the halt came to an end. Notwithstanding the fact that the column had opened out, each Battalion marching at a lateral distance of several hundred yards, the dust nuisance became as acute as ever. Some men cursed the elements aloud; others trudged along in pained silence hoping against hope that the phantom wire road would make its appearance and effect for them a timely rescue from suffocation.

It was a common sight to see men of the regiments ahead stretched out on the ground with a comrade in attendance. These poor fellows, unable to endure the strain, and overcome by fatigue, had perforce to fall out and chance being picked up by the Field Ambulance that followed in the rear, failing which they would have to struggle along independently as and when their strength returned.

The following day we were gratified to learn that the second stage of the march, that from Sheikh Nuran, was to be carried out under greatly improved conditions. We were to march " by companies " and by this means it was hoped sufficient space would be allowed between each Company to enable any dust that rose to be dispersed by any breeze there should happen to be.

We also had the additional advantage, very soon after starting, of following a " Motor Road " constructed primarily for the use of motor ambulances conveying sick and wounded from the front line dressing stations or " Aid Posts " to the Stationary Field Ambulances some distance back. The surface sand had been cleared away and banked up on either side of the road. This valuable work was performed by large gangs of the Egyptian Labour Corps, whose further duty it was to keep the roads clear of all loose sand.

Towards nightfall we saw lights through the gloom on either side, denoting the positions of camps, and we then entered a wady enclosed by numerous irregular sandhills.

A battalion marching in the desert at night is strangely silent, the only sound to be heard being the rattle of entrenching-tool helves against bayonets swinging to the motion of the body. The column from a short distance looks more like a great black snake slowly shaping its course over the sand. A broad white belt traversed our path some way ahead, and as the advanced Companies crossed it, the peculiar crunching sound caused by walking on shingle was sharply contrasted to the previous silence. The white belt shown up so distinctly by the brilliant moonlight was the bed of the Wady Ghuzzeh, along the farther bank of which the British front-line positions were established. The actual wady bed varies from fifty to one hundred yards in width, but there are overflow banks extending in places to a depth of one thousand yards which have been peculiarly cut up by the rushing torrents of past ages.

We crossed the wady and penetrated amongst the maze of hillocks on the opposite side. Two Companies of our Battalion proceeded immediately to the positions and took over from a Battalion of the 53rd (Welsh) Division.

This point of the Wady Ghuzzeh is called Shellal, though there is absolutely no sign of habitation or other characteristic warranting its having a name at all. The course of the wady marks the limit of the sand zone.

The line here was indeed a simple one. A system of redoubts had been constructed at a distance of some five hundred yards apart, each being manned by a platoon. During the day an observation post of an N.C.O. and four men only was maintained at each redoubt, but at night the whole platoon was on duty, supplying from four to six posts, including the listening posts situated at gaps in the single belt of barbed wire which protected the whole front. The deep wady in rear afforded excellent natural cover for a whole army, though with the introduction of aerial observation into modern warfare the advantages of this important characteristic were considerably diminished.

It was very difficult to get much sleep in the daytime owing to the heat and the swarms of flies that intruded into our blanket bivouacs. In order to get any sleep at all it was necessary to protect completely all bare parts of the body, using the square yard of mosquito netting which was issued to cover over the head, and a towel or spare shirt over arms and knees. Even then, by so wrapping up, the heat became the more trying and sleep improbable.

In accordance with the intention before mentioned,

we were the extreme right Battalion, our flank being protected by strong cavalry patrols of the Australian Light Horse and certain Regiments of County Yeomanry. The enemy's left flank at Beersheba was approximately fifteen miles away, the two lines converging towards Gaza, where the comparatively close proximity of the respective positions permitted trench warfare.

The country in front of Shellal was a barren wilderness, sparsely covered with coarse dried-up grass with an occasional stunted bush, but the general aspect was extremely desolate. The monotony of the day posts was intensified considerably by this uninteresting landscape. One would stand for two hours at a stretch with no shelter from the hot sun but that afforded by a pith helmet, and gaze into the dreary waste thinking of anything but Turks and war.

To the right all sorts of wonderful tricks are being played upon the imagination. A clump of dark trees appears growing on the brink of a lake, upon whose shining waters the sun's powerful reflection shows up bright and dazzling, the whole scene scintillating in the heated atmosphere. You marvel at not having noticed the comparative beauty before, but on second thoughts remember that it is only a mirage, a pure hallucination. You can readily understand how it is that travellers are so easily deceived, being lured on, and still farther on into the desert by such presumably shady oases offering water to man and beast, only to meet with bitter disappointment and very often death.

Your gaze travels farther round, and in front of you, somewhere across the flat country, a low ridge of hills looms up through the haze. These must be quite near Beersheba, perhaps the Turkish positions themselves! " What sort of men are occupying them," you wonder, " and by what chain of events will they be reached and passed?" These thoughts into the uncertain future are probably promoted by the gradual appearance, as the brilliancy of the sun dies, of the blue contour of another ridge of greater altitude and very much farther away. You speculate as to the distance and identity of this fresh object of interest, and bringing your imagination into full play, paint various pictures of the intervening country and its inhabitants. Surely this second ridge must be the southern fringe of the Judean Hills! The very name turns your thoughts to Biblical history, so wonderfully vague, yet so very authentic. Will you ever reach the country now dimly visible, yet in sight, wherein your religion has its foundation? What victories will have to be won, and what hardships and privations borne, before it is reached? And so your thoughts travel on until you are awakened from your reverie by suddenly detecting, far away in front, a small cloud of dust—a mere grey puff. You are at once all attention, welcoming any event, however small, to create a diversion from the monotony of your virgil. There can be but two reasons for that cloud of dust, i.e., a whirlwind, or a disturbance made by some animate object. The first of these is at once negatived, for the dust does not rise sufficiently high or travel fast enough to owe its origin to such a cause. The second, then, remains, and with it interest increases.

Through your field-glasses (which are part of the equipment of the post) you can faintly distinguish two figures, small dark specks showing up against the dust and therefore travelling towards you. Two figures! No, there must be more; sometimes parted and then as if merged into one. Again you look, and decide that there *are* four; but the scintillation caused by the heat makes it very difficult to be certain at such a distance. Half an hour passes and closer observation proves them to be three figures, thicker at the base than at the top—obviously horsemen. On they come, making straight for a gap in the wire, which shows they are acquainted with the route. Who can they be? They are riding abreast at an easy trot, as though their horses are weary with the distance they had come. The centre figure appears differently clad from those on each side.

As the horsemen draw nearer the outside riders are easily recognized as two powerfully-built, sun-bronzed members of that picturesque body the " Australian Light Horse." Their companion proves to be a Turkish cavalryman taken prisoner, maybe, whilst engaged upon some scouting manœuvre. They pass through the gap, dismount, and an N.C.O. and two men from the nearest post meet them. After a few minutes' conversation the prisoner is duly handed over, one man taking his horse, another motioning him to follow, and the party proceeds to Battalion Headquarters.

Meanwhile the captors, being relieved of their encumbrance, mount their steeds, turn their heads again to the wilderness from which they have just come, and at an easy pace return to rejoin their patrol.

Such incidents were of frequent occurrence. Generally the prisoners were Turkish infantrymen who, having resolved to desert and make their way into our lines, had lost themselves and been found in a half-starved condition by one of the mounted patrols.

Of an evening it was a magnificent sight to see the

cavalry going out in whole Squadrons, or perhaps Regiments, according to the operations in hand, incurring the envy of the defenders of dreary old redoubts who had nothing more exciting to look forward to than an issue of tea at " stand to."

CHAPTER VII

THE ADVANCE COMMENCES (*August, September, October,* 1917)

OUR Brigade was relieved by another of the Division and we repaired to El' Sho'uth, a collection of " cactus gardens " about four miles behind the line. These gardens were merely small enclosures of about two acres in area harbouring a few weeds and shrubs and bounded by hedges of cactus. A system of trenches had been constructed on the northern and western sides by the Turks during their term of occupation, which were cunningly protected by numerous cavalry pits dug so close together that no horse could negotiate them without meeting disaster. They would also have proved a very formidable obstacle to Infantry unaware of their existence.

Information began to leak out that an advance was contemplated as soon as the hot weather had passed, and this was substantiated by a strenuous programme of training comprising, *inter alia,* long night marches followed by elaborate schemes of attack. As one of the Battalion Scouts I found the former particularly interesting. Direction was obtained entirely by compass, and of course the onus rested upon the scouts to lead the Battalion or Company by the most direct route. Sometimes we were away in the desert for three or four days at a stretch.

Shortly before high noon every day a hot wind commenced to blow and continued until sunset, being accelerated by strong gusts that always seemed to rise at most vital moments. For instance, a meal would be ready by about four o'clock, and just as it was being served along came a particularly powerful gust spraying everything, including the dinner, with a covering of fine sand. The cooks need never have feared lest the stew should not be thick enough, for substance was thus quickly added. It was inadvisable to leave articles of clothing spread out on the sand, perhaps to air, for there was a danger of their never being found again. I once laid out my kilt in the manner suggested, and upon looking for it later could find no trace of it. The missing article was produced later by a friend, who said that it was completely covered by drift sand, but in walking past my blanket bivouac he had caught his foot in it and so rescued it for me.

We knew how to appreciate a drop of water in Sinai. Our water was brought to us in rectangular tanks (*fanatis*). A dozen or so camels with their native drivers (" Camel Transport Corps ") were attached to each Battalion and made two journeys per day to the Wady Ghuzzeh, where the engineers had sunk wells and constructed a huge reservoir. The official allowance was two quarts per man per day, one for drinking and one for cooking, but on the subject of washing silence was observed. It went hard, however, with any man who failed to shave daily. What water there was left after bottles had been filled was emptied into any available receptacles and used for washing purposes. A man would indulge in the luxury of a " bath " in about three pints of water, after which he would wash any soiled articles of apparel he had, and even then the " water " would be bespoken after him by some other believer, until the remains were really beyond further use.

The time for the advance in which we were to take part was definitely fixed for the end of October, and when that month arrived preparations were commenced. Bivouacking paraphernalia was re-issued together with an extra water-bottle and a bottle of water-purifying tablets.

I well remember when I was a small boy and the South African War was visited upon us like an endemic disease, how impressed my youthful mind was upon being told by a playfellow that our soldiers were sharpening their swords. These thoughts of my childhood were clearly recalled now that our bayonets were being sharpened by the engineers for the grim work before us.

A few enthusiasts set the fashion by having their hair cropped clean, whereupon the whole Battalion, with few exceptions, followed suit. Many were the luxurious heads of hair temporarily ruined by the merciless hand of some bald-headed tyrant who, with the Platoon's hair-clippers, operated upon the hirsute cranium of a friend, experiencing a fiendish delight in the work of destruction upon which he was engaged. Good progress would be made and one half of the patient's head completely bald when the machine, having swallowed more of the sand that unavoidably gathers in the hair than it could digest, gave a sudden choke and refused to continue its work. This necessitated half an hour's careful cleaning, what time the half bald warrior would be subjected by his friends to uncomplimentary remarks which are best left to the imagination.

Our Division was to attack and take the Beersheba

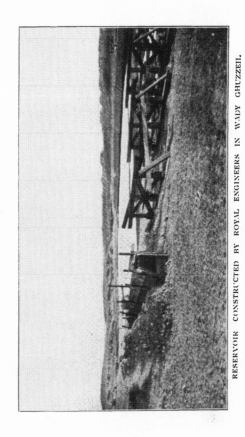

RESERVOIR CONSTRUCTED BY ROYAL ENGINEERS IN WADY GHUZZEH.

defences, and our Battalion would be in the attacking
line on the eventful day.

I was engaged with a colleague upon preparing
maps of these defences, enlarging the official ones
supplied and augmenting them with the latest
information obtained by aerial reconnaissance.   It
was an elaborate map, carefully drawn and minutely
co-ordinated, and the Colonel ordered enough copies
to supply all Company and Platoon Commanders and
specialist officers.   It was fascinating work committing
to paper in our quiet desert home positions many miles
away which we would first see in the turmoil of battle.

Needless to say wheeled transport is useless for
practical purposes in the desert.   That wonderful
animal the camel, therefore, is brought into requisition,
and without him a desert campaign is practically
impossible.   The " Camel Transport Corps," recruited
both as to men and beasts from Egypt and the Sudan,
was a most important wheel in the gigantic military
machine which had been here set in motion, and was
fast gaining speed.   Their camps consisted of a few
bell tents housing the British Officers and staff of
Arabic-speaking soldiers, and hundreds of camels
" barracked " in long straight lines.   A chain ran the
length of each line, to which the camels were fastened.
The native attendants are called " camel drivers."
This is a misnomer, for I have never yet seen a pack
camel being driven, and not only do the " drivers "
always walk in front, but invariably have to pull the
beasts after them.

A company of the " Camel Transport Corps "
would supply camels to a Brigade.   'A certain
number were reserved for carrying water from the
point of supply to Units, while the remainder—those
that were not on the sick list—were held in readiness

for ordinary transport work. When occasion arose calling for the employment of camels a man was sent to the camp, and upon presenting his credentials to the officer in charge, the required number were handed over complete with one " driver " to every pair, and he generally had to give a receipt for both men and camels.

Loading camels is an operation demanding a great deal of patience and not a little skill. The " driver," making a peculiar hissing noise in his throat, drags the camel's head to the ground, whereupon, if the brute is in a good humour, he drops on to his foreknees, his hind legs collapse in sections, and with a lurch forward and another backwards he wriggles himself comfortable in the sand with his long legs doubled up beneath him. He is then ready for loading. It is marvellous how much a camel can carry; he will growl protests with every fresh piece of baggage, but a tender heart would never accomplish the task in hand. Supposing the load to consist of blankets rolled in bundles of ten, there would be, say, six rolls on either side, and having satisfactorily balanced each side load, a nice heavy box would be found to ride in the centre. You wonder whether the animal will ever be able to rise under such a weight, but he reassures you by getting up before you are ready—taking your breath away as you think the load will be pitched off—and walks round. He towers above you like the side of a house, and looks down upon you with a supercilious air, as much as to say, " Ah! you did not think I could manage this little lot, did you? But we camels are really very wonderful." In this respect they undoubtedly are.

It was strictly forbidden to ride upon the camels, so opportunities in this direction were denied us.

Professor Palmer describes his first camel ride as follows: " The camel is a much overrated beast, and is the very incarnation of peevish ill-temper. Docile he is, but apparently from no other reason than sheer stupidity. No sooner do you approach him than he sets up a hideous snarling groan; the driver pulls his head forcibly down to the ground, and you seize the opportunity of jumping on to his back. But before you can secure your seat you are suddenly pitched violently forward, then as violently backward, for the creature gets up by jerks, and only half of him at a time. When once mounted the motion is not so unpleasant as it has been described, and in a very few days makes you quite at home in your elevated seat."

In due course all preparations for leaving our cactus garden home were completed. We packed all surplus kit and articles of personal property in carefully labelled sandbags and committed them to the care of the " Q.M." stores. Only the bare necessities were to be carried. It is a mere matter of detail that we never saw those sandbags or their contents again.

My colleague and I had to map out the route to a given co-ordinate, supplying the compass bearings and distances in yards from point to point. The distances would be paced out according to formula by scouts marching at the head of the column, and one evening, shortly before dusk, we set out upon our adventures.

Following in the rear of each Company were pack mules loaded with the Lewis guns and ammunition, and following in the rear of the Battalion were more mules and a number of camels carrying the reserve supply of ammunition and a very limited quantity of baggage, such as medical stores, spare stretchers, and sanitary paraphernalia. The water camels and those for carrying rations (which were to make daily journeys to the Units), and the remainder of the pack transport, were brigaded and would follow independently in the wake of the advance.

At the point of Brigade Concentration, General Shea, our Division Commander, made a short speech, the whole Brigade gathering round him in one huge crowd at his request.

The time for sentiment was now past, and we proceeded to the great Wady Ghuzzeh, which we crossed at Gamli, a spot farther south than we had yet been, and there camped.

The next evening we resumed, following the wady on the northern bank. We were virtually in "No Man's Land," but there were fifteen miles of it in width; and what a different "No Man's Land" from those of France and Macedonia, which now lay quite dim in the seclusion of our memories!

Still farther south the wady forked, one branch continuing in the general direction, and another issuing from the east. The latter was the Wady Essani, a few miles along which we reached our destination for that night. Three Companies moved forward and established an outpost line, while the fourth remained in reserve concealed in a small wady near Battalion Headquarters.

This locality took its name from the Wady Essani. We remained there for four or five days, during which time fresh information concerning the enemy's positions arrived from higher headquarters in a regular stream, and which had, of course, to be shown on all the maps in the Battalion, giving us " mappers " a deal of trouble.

Owing probably to my useful knowledge of

topography in general and maps in particular, I was appointed to be general factotum to the Colonel, a sort of aide-de-camp, and was always to accompany him during the advance—of course, at a respectful distance in the rear.   It was due to that fact that I had such favourable opportunities and points of vantage afforded me to obtain a comprehensive view of the operations.

One morning at Essani a man from one of the outposts came in to Battalion Headquarters escorting what appeared to be a party of four or five women. On closer inspection this little procession proved to consist of one old Arab, a very old Arab woman, two younger women, one small girl, and a dog.   They were dressed in filthy rags, and were in a very emaciated condition.   The dog, a nondescript whelp, was the best nourished amongst them.   They moved very slowly and painfully, and eventually reached the camp, casting furtive glances mingled with fear and suspicion at our men.   Heaven knows where they had come from or how long they had been wandering about homeless and foodless!   No sooner had they stopped than the old woman fell to the ground shrieking and flinging her arms and legs about.   Her companions appeared quite unconcerned, as if whether she lived or died was a matter of indifference to them; or perhaps they were beyond all feeling.   If she had been a white woman I should have diagnosed hysterics, but I really do not know if such an old hag could be capable of so feminine a complaint.

However, the doctor arrived upon the scene and endeavoured to administer a stimulant, but she would have none of it.   She refused to be touched; and her friends continued in their state of apathy.   Eventually the old woman was borne away on a stretcher; the

E

others followed, and this procession of abject misery moved slowly away to be interrogated by the proper authority, when it would be decided whether the vagrants should be treated as prisoners or refugees.

We left Essani one night, departed from the course of the wady, and marched across country to Abu Ghalyun.   There was nothing at Abu Ghalyun but another wady with precipitous sides, in which we camped.   " Abu " means " Father of," but who Ghalyun was nobody seemed to know.

The following day was a Sunday, and a Church Service was held, at which the Colonel addressed the Battalion to the effect that we were about to come to grips with the Turks, who were acknowledged to be fine fighters, and emphasizing the fact that we should not in any way commit the error of under-estimating our enemy.   We were by far the better equipped force, but nevertheless there was undoubtedly a hard time before us, when we should be called upon to make still greater sacrifices than had been yet demanded of us, etc., etc.

During the afternoon final preparations were made, each man was given two bombs and an extra bandolier of ammunition.   A percentage were given coloured flare-lights to be used as locating signals to aeroplanes, while others carried wire-cutters and circular saws. Forty-eight hours' rations were issued, consisting of bully beef, biscuits, jam, and dried fruit, together with a small bottle of tea and rum.   A hot meal was served; the last we were to have from the cooks for many weeks.   The camp was cleared up, everything packed, and we made ready to start.   We were to be in position by midnight, and the attack was to be launched at dawn.

Certain valuable persons, including craftsmen and

(*Upper*) TRANSPORT CAMELS BARRACKED.
(*Lower*) READY FOR THE DAY'S WORK.

the Company quartermasters, were formed into a
rear party called " C. Echelon," and they were to be
responsible for bringing along the rations and water
every day. A " B. Echelon " was formed under the
Battalion Sergeant-Major in charge of the ammunition
mules.

We set out at dusk, our course lying still to the
south-east. A wire road, the first and last that we
encountered, had been specially constructed over a
particularly heavy stretch of sand, but our excitement
was intense, and we did not need it, for our old bug-
bear, Fatigue, was a stranger to us that night.

After about three miles we bore round to the north
and joined the road leading from the ruined town of
Khalassah (Elusa) to Beersheba.

The landscape was brilliantly lit by the moon, and
the desert highway was strewn here and there with
skeletons, the whole scene looking for all the world like
a stage setting upon which the operator had turned
a pale, cold limelight.   Was it a bad omen?   Yet
the occasion invited such thoughts and set lively
imaginations at work.

Entrenching-tool helves had been tied to bayonet
scabbards to prevent them rattling, and except for
necessary orders uttered in an undertone, no man
spoke.   We were very silent.   The occasional cry of
a jackal and the monotonous chirping of crickets
alone disturbed the stillness of the night.

As we descended the slope of a hill the head of
the column suddenly disappeared like a snake entering
a hole.   It had entered the Wady Martabah, which
crossed our path.   Presently we arrived at the spot
and disappeared too.   We also crossed the shingly bed.
Good God, what a noise!   We negotiated the pebbles
as though they were eggs, and it sounded like ten

thousand contractors' tip-carts shooting loads of shingle from the height of St. Paul's on to the pavement below.

On the other side we halted, each Company in line, and took off our packs. It seemed like rolling up one's sleeves for a fight. We emerged from the wady and advanced over the undulating ground towards the grey hills before us. Here in the brilliant moonlight, but a mile from the Turkish trenches, our forces were marching into battle—Infantry, Trench Mortar Batteries, Machine Gun Corps, and Artillery, all moving *en masse* to take up their positions ready for the onslaught at dawn.

The ground was covered with loose stones, which caused a great deal of noise—to our disadvantage. It sounded like the distant roar of the surf.

Upon entering the wadies intersecting the hills, the various Companies turned off to their respective positions, as several shots rang out, indicating that the enemy were alive to our presence. It was impossible to tell from which particular locality the shots came, but it was practically certain that the Turks had had outposts stationed some considerable distance in front of their trenches which had withdrawn upon our approach.

Our maps proved to be very true, and no difficulty was experienced in identifying the different hills and wadies, and in obtaining a comprehensive idea of the neighbourhood.

The intermittent firing developed into a veritable fusillade, though it proved more disconcerting than effective. Occasionally a gun would roar out, sending a shell shrieking over our heads in search of our own batteries, which could be heard rumbling into position.

A telephone was established in a ditch at Battalion

Headquarters, and ground lines were laid to the Companies.

Everything was carried out according to plan, and there we had to lie in enforced idleness to await dawn. Not a shot was to be fired, and this lack of response on our part seemed to urge the Turks to greater efforts, for they kept up an incessant hail of bullets the whole night long, their machine guns sweeping the slopes of the hills, and their snipers searching the wadies in which we were secluded.

CHAPTER VIII

THE STORMING AND TAKING OF BEERSHEBA

TEN Divisions is a very useful force, especially when under competent generalship. Of course, technically, a General should not be otherwise than competent, though sometimes the skill in military science of those placed in command is unfortunately not all that could be desired.

The plea set up after a military operation that the materials were inadequate is no excuse for the failure of that operation, if it but wanted courageous insistence for the sufficient quantity of materials to be forthcoming. Wars have to be lost by the one side to be won by the other, and we learn by making mistakes; but the price for mistakes in war cannot be paid in gold. If we accept the principles of war, then, it behoves those responsible, when the lives of others are at stake, to make doubly sure that their human tools are sufficiently supported in the struggle so that the result may show a good return for the sacrifices made.

General Allenby, as he then was, had taken over command of the British Expeditionary Force the previous June, and realizing the enormity of his task, stated his requirements, demanding enough men, guns and stores to ensure success. Troops were sent from France, Macedonia, and India to augment the original force, and supplies of every description were dispatched to the railheads during many months previously. Well-conceived plans gradually ripened, and in October, 1917, were ready for putting into execution. Turkish prisoners had stated that they expected us to attack sooner or later, but did not count upon those expectations being realized as soon as they were.

Throughout the advance into Palestine General Allenby's thrusts were characteristic in always being directed against those points of the Turkish line which it was most reasonable to consider immune. This feature, coupled with the masterful handling of cavalry, undoubtedly went far to achieve a success beyond all expectations. Gaza was the most strongly fortified part of the whole enemy's front and was looked upon as the front door and only access to Palestine. It is not surprising, therefore, that the Turk was rather nonplussed and very unprepared when, on the night of October 30th, an Allied host advanced against the side door of Beersheba and spent the night secluded in the wadies beneath his very nose.

The Divisions engaged in the advance were the 10th (Irish), the 52nd (Scottish) on the coast, the 53rd (Welsh), the 54th (Eastern Counties), the 60th (London) on the extreme right, the 74th (dismounted Yeomanry), the 75th (West of England and Indian Troops), two Divisions of Australian and New Zealand Cavalry and the Yeomanry Mounted Division together with the Imperial Camel Corps. Later on (after Jerusalem), the 3rd Lahore and 7th (Indian) Divisions arrived from Mesopotamia to replace some of these Divisions, which were sent, for the second time, to France.

October 31st, 1917.

The initial blow in this great Crusade which was to mark the commencement of a new epoch took place at Beersheba, and that blow, as already stated, was to be struck by our Division at dawn.   On our left was a very formidable salient designated on the maps as the " Z " system of trenches, and before we could advance it was imperative that this salient should fall.   It was opposed by another Brigade in our Division.   At 6 a.m. on the eve of All Hallows, our guns started a slow bombardment of the " Z " salient, gradually increasing until it became intense. After being harassed all night by Turkish rifle and machine-gun bullets and the fitful screeching of the enemy's guns, the methodical barking of our own batteries sounded like sweet music as the reports merged into one continuous roar which rolled through the air to lose itself in the winding wadies.   Suddenly the bombardment ceased, giving way to the rattle of rifle, Lewis gun and machine-gun fire, and we knew that our comrades on the left had " gone over."

The fight must have been short and swift, for we soon had word that the " Z " salient had been taken. It was our turn next.   The front line Companies arranged themselves in sections of bombers, grenadiers, riflemen and Lewis gunners, for each section would advance as a " blob " fifty yards from the next on either side.   The attack formation was in waves of sections or " blobs," and there were to be two Companies in the front line, one in support and one in reserve.

As the morning wore on the sun became very hot and we dared not drink beyond moistening the lips, for although our bottles were full we did not know when we should get them replenished.

Several men had been wounded during the night and a few killed. Periodically a stretcher-bearing party would slowly make its way over the difficult ground, carrying the wounded to the dressing station, where they were laid in a row in any shade that could be contrived for them until they could be attended to.

We waited half an hour, one hour, two hours, and still the word to advance was not given by Brigade Headquarters. True, the firing on the left still continued, so perhaps the Turks were counter-attacking. And yet we waited; the enemy in front of us continuing to sweep the intervening ridges with their machine-gun fire. The desire to be " up and at 'em " was general; anything but this suspense !

Suddenly a gun boomed out from directly behind us, then another, being followed in quick succession by the batteries on our right and left. Thank heaven it would not be long now ! The guns had swung round and were directing their attention to our front. How they banged away at those trenches ! The vibration shook the very ground upon which we stood. There surely would be nothing left for us to attack when we reached the objective; but that the Turks were still in possession was evidenced by the hail of bullets that came from their direction.

In a few more minutes the " zero " would be reached, the guns lift, and we would advance. The Colonel made towards the attacking Companies, myself in attendance. All was ready, bayonets fixed, magazines filled, and the men of the first wave crouched just below the sky-line of the ridge wait-ing for the signal to go forward—and God knows where else. Their faces were a study, and in them could be read a mixture of curiosity, alarm and expectation.

Amid the din a voice roared out. All eyes were turned to the Company Commander, a thick-set swarthy Scot, as he swung his arm forward above his head giving the signal to advance. The men moved forward and gained the crest. That was the psychological moment. I fully expected to see them shot down like flies, but not a man was hit. As each approached, a keen observer would have faintly distinguished a momentary falter, a mere semblance to hesitation as though preparing to receive a shock —but that was all. In a flash it had passed, the man was on the sky-line, and reassured by seeing his comrades descending the hill unhurt before him, he, too, pushed forward and was lost to view. The first and second waves had disappeared, and the Colonel could hold back no longer. He motioned me to follow, and set off at a quick pace down the wady side.

In order that the Colonel's position could be seen easily during the operation I carried a " Scottish Standard " fastened to a staff. With this and other impedimenta I followed with what speed the loose, stony surface and the steep gradient would allow. Down the slope we hurried, jumped the ditch at the bottom, and up the other side. Here we were confronted by another similar wady running parallel to the enemy's trenches which were on the farther crest. A glance showed that the first wave was ascending the slope and preparing for the final assault, but beyond that I could take in no other particulars, for the next moment a rocky projection cut them out of view. The Colonel hurried down the hill with the rampant lion fluttering at as short a distance in the rear as its panting bearer could reasonably be expected to maintain.

We passed through the second wave, which had now extended in open order, and pressed on up the final slope. Would we be in time to take part in the assault, for already a shouting and commotion could be heard? We still had fifty yards to go when a figure, clad in some blue cotton garb, came running down the hill making in our direction. He sank to his knees before the Colonel, clutched at his tunic, kissed it, and raising his large terror-stricken eyes in appeal, gabbled some unintelligible sentences in which "Allah" was accorded chief prominence. He appeared to be an Arab, and no doubt was one of the thousands of unfortunates who had been pressed into fighting for a Monarchy which they neither acknowledged nor respected. He was dragged to his feet by a muscular corporal and taken away.

The leading wave was occupying the trenches, but the Turks had flown. They had had their fill with the bombardment and elected not to wait for a hand-to-hand encounter.

By this time the supports and reserves had passed through the attacking line, and were consolidating about two hundred yards forward.

The Turkish trenches were dug in hard chalky ground, and were of an average depth of but four and a half feet. In them was a litter of equipment and ammunition (mostly German), ragged articles of clothing of various colours (essentially Oriental), and a few recumbent Turkish figures. Upon the faces of them all was the stamp of death. But what was this? A gurgling sound as of laboured breathing emanated from one figure huddled up on the bottom of the trench. He was unconscious and in a deplorable condition, with his right jaw blown away and one foot hanging by a thread, besides other minor injuries. The doctor was too busy tending our own casualties to pay any heed to this poor fellow, but a humane heart saw to it that his agonies were cut short and the journey to his Maker facilitated.

Situated in dead ground behind the trenches was the Turks' camp. The officers' tents and the men's bivouacs were still standing, with their contents just as the occupants had left them when the alarm was given the night before. Apparently nothing had been removed. With these facts in view, the success of the surprise attack need not be dwelt upon.

The Turks had naturally chosen the highest ground amid the hills upon which to construct their defences. From this point of vantage the landscape away to the North presented to the observer a barren grey-brown expanse, the only relief being created by the village of Beersheba, whose white square houses were gathered together, as if for companionship's sake, in a hollow about two miles distant. Beyond the village, the country rolled away in undulations culminating in the hills of Southern Judea.

Fleeing towards Beersheba were small parties of the enemy with our Reserve Battalion in hot pursuit. The Australian cavalry were also making an encircling movement from the right in order to cut off the fugitives' flight. Several hundreds were rounded up like so many cattle in and around the village.

The Turkish artillerymen had managed to get their guns away, and at this juncture disposed of their spare ammunition by the efficacious method of dispatching it piecemeal to their late positions, where our men were consolidating. A machine gun cunningly concealed somewhere among the dunes, also opened fire, inflicting some casualties.

Towards dusk all was quiet, and after clearing out the trenches we settled down to spend the night in them. The ration and water convoy arrived, as also did the Battalion baggage with our packs, which in future were to burden our progress.

Salvage parties were sent out the next day, and many men returned with Turkish waistcoats, scarves and woollen gloves, all of brilliant and various colours, with which they adorned themselves and created not a little amusement by their antics. Some fortunate fellows managed to find a quantity of Turkish tobacco, really poor stuff, but as there was scarcely a cigarette or an ounce of tobacco in the Battalion, it can be imagined with what eagerness it was secured. Inveterate smokers were reduced to smoking tea leaves. Having made their mess-tin of tea, they carefully spread the leaves out upon a piece of paper in the sun to dry, and afterwards persuaded themselves that they derived pleasure from smoking them. Such was the extent to which the smoking habit had grown upon us; it smelt like a gardener's fire at home during the deciduous period. But that was not the lowest rung of the retrogressional ladder, which is so easy of descent where men are leading unnatural lives and are confronted by unusual hardships. The one-time followers of Boadicea or Joan of Arc are reduced to a negligible number when compared with the slaving multitudes of " Lady Nicotine." It may seem incredible to you, good reader, and you may throw up your hands in disgust at the very thought, but it is nevertheless true that during the early days of the Palestine advance some men, in their endeavours to satiate their craving for tobacco, attempted to smoke camel manure. The experiment proved a failure as it well need have done, and the incorrigibles were constrained to persevere with tea leaves. It was really pitiable to see them going about begging them from others.

Of the many private and public bodies which had undertaken the task of supplying the troops with smoking materials, how many, I wonder, realized that men were ever in such a predicament as we were at Beersheba? A small quantity of these luxuries which custom and long usage have made necessities would indeed have been an unexpected piece of good fortune.

CHAPTER IX

BEERSHEBA, or Bir-es-seba, " The Well of the Oath," is the site where Abraham dug the well and made the covenant with Abimelech. Here Abraham dwelt, and in this neighbourhood Ishmael and Isaac were born, so it can be said that Beersheba is one of the oldest sites, if not the oldest, in Biblical history that can be authenticated. There stands to-day, built round two of the seven wells for which it was famous, a village bearing the same name as that of Abraham's time. That patriarch also planted a grove at Beersheba, but it must have been very different then from the same place now. The two wells existing to-day still produce water, though it is hard to conceive that this parched, barren land could produce anything moist at all, let alone water. At the particular time of the year of which I write, after the long, dry summer, the entire absence of tree or shrub, or, in fact, any vegetation whatever, created a most depressing scene. Strange thoughts are inspired in the observer as he contemplates the desolation before him, if he but dwells for a moment upon the old associations of the place. Somewhere in this neighbourhood Esau sold his birthright for a mess of pottage of bread and lentils, and as you gaze upon the wilderness in which this took place about 1805 B.C., and bear in mind the fact that he was on the verge of starvation, you do not altogether wonder at it. The desolation and loneliness are so intense as to be almost felt as tangible things.

The majority of Arabic names can be translated, such as in the case of "Beersheba." The troops who captured that place and know its "attractions" soon found their own facetious translation, however, i.e., Beer, the same as in English: sheba, "nothing doing."

On November 7th Gaza fell. The surprise attack at Beersheba had been followed immediately by a terrific onslaught against the enemy's stronghold on the coast. The defences were taken and the Turks retired in disorder, being harassed from the sea by the guns of Allied warships, and from the skies by a merciless rain of bombs and machine-gun fire from our aeroplanes.

To add to their troubles, the cavalry were pressing hard upon their heels, rounding up thousands of prisoners among the sand-dunes and cactus plantations that are to be found to the north of Gaza, so that with both flanks in the air the Turks had no alternative but to fall back in the centre. It was a complete *débâcle*. On the left they were given no peace as our troops tenaciously drove on north-wards. On the right our progress was not quite so rapid. The 53rd Division proceeded to Dhaheriyeh, and thence along the Hebron road. The cavalry had pressed on past Muweileh, in the Irgeig district, to Kauwukah, where an elaborate defence system (the Rushdi System) had been constructed. The military railway here bends round on its way from Jaffa to Beersheba, passing over a broad wady by a five-arch stone bridge. These positions were occupied by a very strong Turkish rearguard, which was expected to put up a determined resistance.

Towards these defences, then, we marched, passing through Beersheba itself. Like all Arab villages, it looked quite clean and picturesque from a distance, but upon closer inspection proved to be filthy in the extreme.

The ground was strewn with refuse, and the air was thick with nauseating odours. The few natives who lived there lounged about their dilapidated dwellings, and stared at us in wide-eyed wonderment, in which could be traced a timid friendliness, as yet strongly influenced by the uncertainty as to whether we were welcome or not. But then, were not their sympathies being gradually and diplomatically transmitted from vanquished oppressors to victorious strangers? The inhabitants of " occupied " territory are ever in that unfortunate predicament until they realize that discretion is the better part of valour and decide to acknowledge the stronger power for the time being. Time, aided by sympathetic treatment and justice, however, soon convinced the Arabs of the wisdom of their decision.

Just as the column emerged from the outskirts of the village, an enemy aeroplane, shielded by the strong rays of the sun, swooped silently down from the sky and attempted to bomb us. Immediately upon his presence and intention being detected, everybody scattered and prepared to drive him off with rifle fire. Several bombs were dropped, but, as if by the irony of fate, the only casualties inflicted were the killing of some Turkish prisoners who were passing near by.

Several miles over barren, trackless country brought us to a maze of low-lying hills, and

F

under cover of night we camped in the intersecting wadies.

The farther we progressed, the greater the distance our convoys had to travel, for the point of supply could not be moved every day. The capacity of the wells at Beersheba was not sufficient to produce water for everybody, and as wells are very few and far between in this land, many convoys had still to draw from the original source several miles south of Beersheba. Our Brigade convoy was one of these. Consequently, when we camped at Muweileh, we had to lie down to rest with parched throats. After a trying march in the heat, nothing can be a greater hardship than to be without water. The majority of bottles were not absolutely dry, for a wise campaigner never allows such a circumstance to obtain, but, unfortunately, all of us are not gifted with that wisdom which prompts us to provide against contingent events. Some men had not a drop of water left. The full emergency bottle, of course, was sacred.

Water was as necessary to us as rifles and ammunition, though it was only on such occasions as this that the fact was fully realized. The following morning, when the sun rose in the heavens, to beat down upon us, our condition grew worse. Men were lying about under the scant shelter of bivouac sheets, inert and irritable, for a raging thirst, without the means of alleviation, produces an agony of both mind and body, which, happily for us, is not experienced in the general walks of this life. "When *would* the water come?" was the question continually asked; but no answer was given, for none could give it. To sip periodically at the little water one had left was quite ineffective, and was like giving small-arms ammunition to a howitzer gun. I was engaged throughout the day in putting the latest information concerning the enemy's defences upon the Battalion's maps, and felt like drinking the very ink I used. I must admit that occasionally I shook my water-bottle just to hear the rattle of the drain of precious liquid still remaining in it, for the sound was comforting.

Certain philosophers—noble fellows—made light of our troubles, asserting that the water would assuredly arrive sooner or later, so what was the use of worrying? As always, they were correct. About midday the water camels were heard blowing and snorting along the wady, and as they drew nearer the sweetest of all music—the splashing of water in the fanatis—gladdened our ears. It actually splashed; yes, and percolating through the stoppers, trickled down the sides. The highest standard of pleasure to the individual is always governed by the greatest need of the body at a particular time. So it was with us upon the arrival of the water. The gratification of the desire to drink water, however, is partially realized by the knowledge of actual possession. Not that our needs were by any means supposititious, but our thirst, like toothache upon the arrival of the sufferer at the dentist's surgery, diminished to a considerable extent when the water arrived.

The water was duly served out, but only a half issue. Great difficulty had been experienced in obtaining even this small quantity, and the remainder of the party had gone on to another well which the Engineers were repairing, and would not return until the next day. But even the short issue saved us. Men drank eagerly but sparingly, though one " whole-hogger " of my acquaintance disposed of his all in one long draught, on the principle that a good drink is satisfying, whereas the retention of the water led to the temptation to sip continually at it without quenching the thirst. The wisdom and efficacy of this method are, perhaps, open to contention.

As for the men who accompanied the convoys over so many weary miles of desert land, and brought us the necessaries of life, they were indeed heroes. Tired, footsore and themselves thirsty, they arrived with the precious supplies cheerful but worn-out. Very often they had to depart again for the next supply as soon as the camels could be unloaded. Seldom did any of them give in, and then only when forced to do so by physical disability. Blistered feet was the usual trouble, which frequently developed into blood-poisoning. Unless you have likewise suffered, it is difficult to appreciate fully the agonies endured by those men who, with feet raw and excruciatingly painful, still carried on with their work of vital importance.

CHAPTER X

BEFORE dawn the next morning, we emerged from the
" Wady of Thirst " prepared for battle. We were
going into action again, though this time in the
capacity of reserves. The objective was the " Rushdi
System " at Kauwukah. Two hours marching
brought us to the point of deployment, where a full
issue of water was awaiting us.

The attacking Battalions had extended and were
advancing over a wide expanse of open ground leading
to the enemy's positions. His artillery was putting
up a somewhat heavy barrage and our own batteries,
already in position, were bombarding with much
vigour. Our Battalion took no part in the fight, but
waited in what ground cover there was in rear, ready
if wanted. When the attacking troops were within
striking distance, a great rattling of machine gun and
rifle fire commenced, tempered by the " crumping "
of our heavier shells, as they burst amongst the
enemy. To the left could be seen the stone railway
bridge spanning a wady, but all that remained were
the piles connected by the metals, for the arches had
been previously destroyed by our gunners.

As the troops advanced, so the artillery moved
forward in support. We have all seen pictures,
depicting artillery galloping into action, and I do not

suppose I have been alone in thinking that such scenes were the fruit of abnormally developed imagination; but no picture, however vivid, could do justice to the thrilling scene here presented.

I crawled to the summit of a low hillock, and through my field glasses, obtained an excellent view of all that was going on. Away in front, partially obscured by the smoke of bursting shells and almost submerged into the colour of their surroundings, were lines of khaki figures slowly advancing in pairs. Behind them were lines of sections not yet extended, and behind them again, followed the supporting Battalion, also in artillery formation. Here and there upon the ground were figures of men, mules, and horses, some wounded and waiting for help, others beyond help. Working amongst them and exposed to all the dangers of the battle-field were the stretcher-bearers, intent upon their labour of mercy. Just ahead of me in a dip in the ground, a battery of field guns was thundering away in support of those dim khaki figures. When it seemed their firing was most intense, it ceased. In a few seconds dust began to rise, and from out of the dip, a team with gun and limber came at full speed, then another and another, until the whole battery was galloping forward. They were soon observed by the Turkish gunners, who immediately opened fire upon them with remarkable accuracy. Shells were bursting on all sides, and only by a miracle were none of them hit. But there was no deterring; those khaki figures in front had to be backed up. On they dashed, swerving this way and that to avoid shell holes and boulders, at times with only two wheels of the guns engaging the ground, until they reached cover behind another low hill. They swung their guns round, unhitched the teams, unlimbered, and in less than a minute were again belching forth their messages of death as fast as one could count them.

During the morning the battle raged loud and long, and we could not tell how went the day. At noon we moved forward, so undoubtedly good progress had been made.

In the early afternoon, word came that the position had been captured and consolidation was in progress. It had been a tough fight and casualties on both sides were somewhat heavy. The Turks had fallen back upon their next line of defence, and towards evening our aeroplanes were up reconnoitring to confirm this. Somewhere on our right flank the Turkish gunners had not yet taken their departure, and were sending along their respects, or their curses, in the form of ten minutes' rapid firing of shrapnel timed to burst about a hundred feet above the ground. Except for a few slight scratches, no harm was done.

The following day, in order of sequence, we became the reserve Brigade in the Division. We were not moving until midday, so I proceeded to the high ground recently evacuated to take certain bearings, and at the same time had an opportunity of inspecting the trenches. They were deep and well constructed, with tunnels and bridges, and most elaborate machine-gun emplacements, which must have entailed a great deal of labour. Judging from the number of shell holes in and around the works, our bombardment must have been terrific. There had been barbed wire entanglements in front, but very few of them were left standing. In one machine-gun emplacement the gun was still in position, with a half exhausted cartridge belt in the breech, and bending over the weapon was the gunner, still at his post—dead. Bombs, equipment, broken rifles and empty ammunition boxes were all over the place, and lying here and there were the bodies of dead Turks.

At one spot about six bodies had been placed side by side, each reversed to the one next to it, so that along one side they were in the alternate order of head, feet, head, feet, and so on. Hovering over them was a man of one of the attacking Battalions of the previous day, and then evidently on a salvage party. He looked each corpse in the face, now so still and tranquil, his own filled with malignity. He gesticulated wildly, and in a loud voice cursed them. He cursed so, and swore terrible oaths with such emphasis and obvious sincerity, that I began to think him demented. But who can tell what mental suffering he was undergoing—what memories of fallen comrades he carried? Though our enemies, they had made the supreme sacrifice, for such it was, whatever the cause and however mistaken. It did not appear seemly, therefore, that this tirade of malediction should be heaped upon their shattered and lifeless remains.

CHAPTER XI

THE PLAINS OF PHILISTIA (*November*, 1917)

OUR next objective was the Wady Sheria. At one point in the wady, a little to our right, were a few buildings and sheds constituting a railway station with a water supply reputed to be ample for our needs. Naturally enough, animals need water as much as men, and the majority of our horses and mules had not watered for about two days. The artillerymen had been forced to shoot several of their horses, which had collapsed more from the want of water than fatigue. The water supply of Sheria, therefore, was in itself a sufficient objective without taking into consideration the strong tactical position occupied by the enemy on the right bank of the wady.

In spite of the strong resistance of the Turks, the determined and methodical attack by our troops resulted, before dusk, in the capture of Sheria Station, the much coveted water supply in the wady, and the high ground beyond. This was the occasion when the Worcester and Warwick Yeomanry, working on our right, made their famous charge, capturing twelve of the enemy's guns which were firing at point blank range—an achievement not unattended by serious losses on both sides, but the chargers who reached the goal made quite sure that the charged were all accounted for.

89

Towards the afternoon heliographic messages flashed in the powerful sunlight, intimating that the positions were taken, whereupon we set off to relieve the Brigade that had been engaged in the operation. It was necessary in order to reach the Wady Sheria to cross a sandy plain about three miles in width, and, in so doing, we attracted the attention of the Turkish gunners, who subjected us to about an hour's heavy fire, as was their usual custom when retiring. When advancing over an open stretch of country within the " danger zone," artillery formation is adopted with the object of reducing to a minimum the target presented. The formation is carried out by the advancing body proceeding in lines of sections or half platoons (facetiously termed " blobs ") at a distance of fifty to seventy-five yards between each line, the same number of yards separating each " blob." In order to destroy any uniformity of line the " blobs " are just not " covered off " laterally or from front to rear. The officer or N.C.O. in charge rejoiced in the title of " blob commander." After a time we became indifferent to these bouts of firing on the part of the Turks, whose practice was to direct the fire so as to traverse the whole front, though by watching where the shells burst and calculating which particular area was engaging the gunners' attention, the tendency of each " blob " was unconsciously to veer off at a tangent in the opposite direction.

A Division advancing in artillery formation followed by whole convoys of transport stretching back to the sky-line must present a very disconcerting sight to the men endeavouring to arrest its progress, especially when shells make no impression whatever upon the mass gradually and mechanically, but very surely, drawing nearer. Occasionally a party would be obscured by the smoke of an exploding shell, but when the air cleared they would be marching on just as before, except that perhaps one or more of their number would be left lying upon the ground. Their progress could not be arrested, for their very safety depended upon constant movement. I particularly recollect seeing one " blob " marching along when a shell came screeching through the air and dropped immediately at the feet of the leading man, sending a shower of sand in all directions. He fell to his knees, but at once got up and resumed, for, by an act of Providence, the shell was defective and failed to explode. The fate of the party had the shell not been a " dud " hardly bears contemplation.

Upon reaching and crossing the Wady Sheria, the Brigade passed through and relieved the troops who had taken the position. By this time it was dark, and two Companies of both front line Battalions moved forward a thousand yards or so, and formed a line parallel to the wady. Our Colonel visited the forward Companies to superintend the establishment of outposts, with myself in attendance. The ground *en route* was gently undulating, the surface being composed of the fine dust with which the reader is now familiar. There was no moon, and the night seemed unusually still and peaceful after the din of battle during the day. We had not got very far, and the front line troops could hardly have been in position, when suddenly two machine guns raised their voices in an agitated protest against our presence and the air was literally filled with showers of lead. The bullets whistled past our ears, many spitefully striking the ground around our feet, raising innumerable little clouds of dust. Needless to say my thoughts, in perfect harmony with the position, were extremely uncomfortable.   For the Colonel, a professional soldier, I cannot speak, though I do not believe he knew what nerves or fear meant.   There was no alternative but to press on, so, with shoulders hunched and heads bent instinctively forward, we continued on our way.

Our guardian angels were in close attendance that night, for we reached the forward positions unhurt. Here we learned that, after the firing had ceased, the men unexpectedly came upon a trench in which were half a dozen Turks with two machine guns and an enormous quantity of ammunition, which they were doing their utmost to exhaust.   Amongst other casualties one of our best Company Commanders, a favourite with the men, had been severely wounded. A section of bombers approached the trench and the occupants offered to surrender, but the men were in no humour for showing mercy.   A few muffled explosions, followed by cries unto Allah, told that the machine gunners had fired their last rounds on this earth.

The next day we advanced from the Wady Sheria, marching in a north-westerly direction.   The neighbourhood had evidently been a large military centre, for deserted camps were dotted about all over the place and numerous dumps of stores had been hurriedly abandoned.   A large quantity of Turkish cigarettes were found here—not of the popular and expensive brands sold at home, but the kind supplied to the Ottoman troops—of indifferent quality, tapered at one end, similar to those found at Beersheba. These were collected and distributed amongst our Division.

During the morning a halt was called to allow the ration convoy to catch up with us, and water and rations were issued. Just at this time parties of Yeomanry came in from the flanks escorting a promiscuous crowd of prisoners who had given their comrades the slip during the retirement of the night before and had waited until we arrived to give themselves up. The majority were poor specimens of mankind, in a very dirty, neglected condition, and all very thirsty. Their experiences in the desert had taught them to retain possession of their water bottles or some utensil capable of holding water, and at the sight of our water fanatis they almost got out of hand in the manifestations of their needs. " Moya, moya! " they cried, holding forth their bottles and tin cans, whilst gold, silver and nickel coins were produced as inducements to give them drink. They begged, they prayed, and they whined for water, but deaf ears were turned to their supplication until all our men were served. At a sign to arrange themselves in some sort of order, there was a scuffling and a scrambling to be first, but those exhibiting the greater eagerness were firmly thrust to the rear and the weaker ones given precedence. It was pitiable indeed to watch these poor wretches greedily drinking, cherishing each precious drop. Some came for more and it was given them. No one who knows the pain of thirst could have refused. Their dull, lifeless eyes brightened and they looked upon us as their saviours, having delivered them from madness and, maybe, fearful death from thirst. They appeared mighty glad to be in our hands, and to show their gratitude turned out their pockets, giving us Turkish coins and notes and any odd articles they happened to have concealed in their ragged garments. Some of us still retain these as souvenirs.

We took the opportunity during the halt to have breakfast. Little fires were lighted and mess tins of tea made which, with thick biscuits and thin jam, constituted our meal.

Resuming the advance in artillery formation, we passed over a rolling expanse of downs, gradually assuming a mantle of green, coarse grass, which proved refreshing to the eye after the glaring sand of the country we had left behind. Towards midday the enemy's rearguard opened fire from its new position on a ridge of hills in front, but this made no difference; we still advanced. The whole landscape was dotted with khaki " blobs " slowly and methodically pressing forward, the artillery in line with the infantry, and away back as far as the eye could reach followed strings of camels and mules bringing along stores and ammunition. A small village surrounded by cactus hedges—the first we encountered since leaving Beersheba—lay in our path, harbouring a number of Turkish machine guns which were somewhat troublesome. These were soon silenced by the Company acting as screen; the gunners were either killed or taken prisoners, and the enemy's main rearguard again had to pack up and bolt. We were able to follow their line of retreat by the tracks made by the guns. At stages, circular ruts in the ground clearly showed where they had turned their guns in attempting to impede our progress, only to move on again leaving a pile of empty shell cases and boxes behind, which latter were eagerly broken up by our men for firewood. The bodies of dead Turks, mules and ponies, were lying here and there by the way, swollen and made hideous by exposure to the sun, polluting the atmosphere.

Late in the afternoon we reached the neighbourhood of Huj, without having come into further contact with the enemy. The many abandoned dumps of stores and ammunition we came across clearly pointed to the great precipitation with which the retreat had been made.   Huj, a village of a few mud houses, had two days previously been the scene of a fierce encounter between the cavalry and a strong enemy force; but, beyond a litter of rubbish and a few broken wagons, no sign remained of the Turkish occupation. The district was hilly and covered with scrub and lank grass.   From the higher points the blue Mediterranean could be seen shimmering in the sun about ten miles to the west, with an intervening belt of sand-dunes skirting the shore.

The coastal forces had pushed beyond this point, and were continuing their drive northwards.   We had been working diagonally across the front, clearing out the straggling Turks from the right to the left, until, converging with the coast, we came to a halt at Huj. Whilst here, news came that the cavalry had reached Ramleh and Ludd, the ancient Lydda, and had crossed the narrow gauge railway that runs from Jaffa to Jerusalem, thus cutting off the supplies of that city from the coast.   Jaffa fell in due course.   The acquisition of that seaport was invaluable, for instead of the requirements of an army being conveyed by thousands of camels all the way from Gaza, to which place the broad gauge line had been extended, supplies were sent from Alexandria and Port Said by sea.   An extended line of communication is never to be recommended, though, of course, the troops operating on the right flank, in the absence of any other means, had still to depend on convoys as hitherto.

The 53rd Division and a detachment of cavalry were making good progress along the Hebron road, and our centre forces were about to enter the Judean Hills from the west along the Jaffa-Jerusalem road.

Thus it will be seen that the Turkish line had swung round, its left flank acting as a pivot with a kink in the centre endangering the Holy City.   Such progress had never been contemplated, the original intention being to break through the enemy's Gaza-Beersheba line, and advance into Palestine by stages so as to get our troops out of the sand zone.   This success, beyond the wildest imagination, was relentlessly pursued, never allowing the Turks the least opportunity to recover their scattered forces or their broken morale.

Our Brigade was sent, more as a precautionary measure, back into the wilderness to a spot called Tel el Nejile, as bands of nomadic Bedouins in league with the enemy were suspected of lurking in that district with no good object.   Our presence there also served the purpose of forming a link with the force engaged in the Hebron sector.   The only living beings we encountered, however, were those from a number of ostensibly peaceful Bedouin encampments.   These were evidently considered harmless and beyond suspicion, so our stay at Nejile lasted but three or four days.   We marched back to Sheria and proceeded thence west to Gaza.

Gaza is protected on the East by a ridge of sandhills, beneath the shelter of which we camped.   This ancient city, after the terrific bombardment it had suffered from land, sea and air, was then a pile of ruins.   The environs of Gaza, especially to the north, resemble a great park of olive groves, extending some miles before merging into the great rolling plain of Philistia.   To the south-east of the town is the hill of Ali Muntar or " Ali el Muntar."   It was to the summit of this hill, nigh unto Hebron, that Samson carried the gates.   During the two previous futile attempts, and the recent successful attempt to take

Gaza, this hill was the scene of the most fierce and bloody battles of the whole campaign.

The next day we commenced the march northwards across the Philistian plain to the land of Judah. It was now, as we passed along one of the oldest routes in history, the highway between Egypt and Syria, trodden throughout the ages " by Egyptian and Syrian Kings, by Greek and Roman conquerors, by Saracens and Crusaders, and lastly by Napoleon from Egypt and back again," we began to feel that we, too, were Crusaders engaged upon a task similar to that held so sacred by our gallant predecessors of the Middle Ages.

Here in Palestine there could be no empty and fallacious reasons for the war we were waging against the Turks, no selfish aims for commercial supremacy, no " Remember Belgium " and other shibboleths which had so sickened us that they became everyday jokes, but the purest of all motives, which was to restore this land, in which Christ lived and died, to the rule of Christian peoples. Apart from any sense of duty, it seemed to me a privilege to take part in such an undertaking.

To free the Holy Land from a policy of organized murder, a tyranny so awful and despicable as to cause the hearts of the most apathetic to revolt in disgust, was in itself sufficient to urge us to great efforts, to suffer increased hardships without complaint. Such thoughts as these came to me as we plodded along this ancient way, and I could clearly see in my mind Cooper's picture of Richard Cœur de Lion, swinging his great battle-axe above his head, engaged in mortal combat with Saladin at the battle of Ascalon. Then came crowding into my brain the stories of Samson, the struggle between the Philistines and the Israelites

G

until David slew the giant Goliath in the very neighbourhood towards which we were marching.

The absence in the history of Palestine of any prolonged era of prosperity, due to the continuous strife to which the country has been subjected, undoubtedly accounts to a large extent for the existence to-day of so many ancient sites that can be identified with those of the Old Testament. With a uniform system of government and ordinary development, the disappearance of those sites might have followed as a matter of course, whereas at the present time, owing to the general decay that seems to have beset the land, the ruins remain to authenticate the Scriptures and help to provide tumbledown dwellings for the fellahin.

Though Gaza, Ascalon, and Ashdod still exist to-day, they are no longer the flourishing seaports they were in olden days, for each is now separated from the sea by an encroaching belt of sand-dunes several miles wide.   Gath, the ancient inland stronghold of the Philistines and birthplace of Goliath, is now represented by but a few ruins on an isolated hill, some sixteen miles from the coast.

As we penetrated farther into Philistia signs of cultivation were evidenced by the appearance of ploughed patches of ground and fields of maize. Small villages were dotted about amid olive trees and cactus plantations, and the inhabitants stood at the doorways of their mud-built dwellings, evincing the greatest curiosity in our passing.   They appeared very well disposed towards us, for they no doubt realized that we had brought to an end the harsh rule of their Ottoman oppressors and, with it, the disappearance of the pauperizing exactions and heartless plunder of a Government which had dominated the fortunes of Palestine like a black cloud for over four hundred years.

Whole families had gone into hiding in the caves among the hills upon learning that the Turkish retreat was imminent, and many of these crossed our path on the way back to their village homes.   The women carried small children tied upon their backs and drove poor half-starved little donkeys struggling along beneath colossal loads, while the men stalked in lordly Eastern fashion behind.   Sometimes families with their worldly belongings would be riding upon camels so skinny that they looked as though they would fall down in sheer fright if shown a bale of tibbin.

CHAPTER XII

AFTER three days of marching, we crossed the Jaffa-Jerusalem railway near Sejid, and reached Latron, where the road from Jaffa via Ramleh enters a long rugged defile on its way through the Judean mountains to the Holy City. The road is metalled and capable of bearing a deal of heavy vehicular traffic, which was fortunate, for wagon transport again came into use and put it to the test.

Army Service Corps dumps and camps were established on either side of the road, and horse lines occupied nearly every level spot. We turned off the road among the hills and camped upon a piece of ground which had been a maize field in the days before the war. It was so stony that clearing operations were necessary before bivouacs could be pitched —a piece of work for which the native farmer was undoubtedly very thankful.

Upon entering the hills, the road gradually rises by an easy gradient, becoming steeper as it progresses. An infantryman has every reason to remember the qualities and gradients of roads, for they play a part in his campaigning career of primary importance—always supposing, of course, that he is fortunate enough to have roads to march upon.

The hills that rose on either side were extremely rocky, with great overhanging ledges of solid stone, threatening any minute to part company with their foundations and precipitate themselves on to the road below. In places, the hills opened out at the junction of several wadies, forming small areas of flat ground, but these were covered with stones and boulders, rendering them unfit for cultivation.

Following the road for some miles, climbing higher and still higher, we arrived at the village of Kuryet-el-Enab which lies in a hollow among the hills. From the highest point a magnificent view is obtained of the rolling plains of Philistia. Splashes of dark green towards Ludd and Jaffa indicate the positions of dense orange groves which are abundantly productive, old Roman roads show up like long white streaks as they connect village with village, and the shining Mediterranean forms a boundary to the whole panorama. Conforming to the shapes of the hills, the road descends through the village by many tortuous twists and then gradually ascends again on its way to Jerusalem. Passing through the village we camped on the stony backward slope of a hill, being thus protected from the Turkish positions. On the opposite hill in our rear was the village of Beit Nakuba, whilst away to the right, across the road, rose the twin conical-shaped hills with the ruins of Kustul reposing on the one, and the village of Soba adorning the pinnacle of the other, the connecting saddle being covered with olive trees.

Kuryet-el-Enab, or Enab, as we called it for short, the " Village of Grapes," is a very ancient site and " better known as Abu Gosh, the name of a celebrated family of bandit chiefs—once the terror of the neighbourhood, but now reduced to insignificance." There are many conflicting theories as to its scriptural name, but the one given most credence, perhaps, is that it is the ancient Kirjath of Benjamin.   In the Middle Ages the Crusaders, under the impression that Kuryet-el-Enab was the ancient Anathoth, built a fine stone church in the village, which still exists in a very good state of preservation.   The monks of the adjoining monastery make an excellent wine, the virtues of which were soon learned and appreciated by the troops, who bought it by the fanati-full.

The houses of Enab are all constructed of white stone quarried in the vicinity and are built among the olive trees which plentifully clothe the hill slopes. The hills of Palestine have a very peculiar appearance on first sight, for by the natural stratification of the rock, they rise in regular ledges or terraces which materially assist the topographer in determining their contour, especially when the view is taken from a neighbouring height.   These terraces are frequently cultivated for the growth of vines, fig and olive trees, though the latter are very common and might be analogized to the oak or chestnut of England.

During the day the sun was quite warm, though the nights and early mornings were very chilly.   A clear cold moon illuminated the landscape, and at night the chimes of Jerusalem could be faintly heard as they were wafted over the hills by a gentle breeze. How wonderful it seemed to be within so short a distance of the Holiest City in the World—and yet not see it!   But we should see it, most of us, and very soon, as preparations for the attack on the Turkish defences were already in progress.

Maps had to be prepared, enlarged and duplicated, and intelligence reports were studied for information concerning the enemy's positions.   Our Colonel was not satisfied with the official maps supplied which, apart from being inaccurate in many particulars, were very unwieldy to handle in action. Upon their foundation, however, my colleague and I prepared fresh maps, augmented and kept up to date by reports from our own observation posts and the official reports. Panoramic " field sketches " were also required, and these we drew on large slips of paper horizontally, showing the actual trenches or sangars occupied by the Turks, and giving ranges and compass bearings from the point of observation, together with any other particulars as to numerical strength of posts that could be ascertained.

Needless to say we gloried in doing this work as a welcome change from the tedious monotony of ordinary duty and made rather a speciality of it, earning something of a reputation in the Division. Curious as it may seem, there is no official status for a " Mapper " in an infantry unit, and although there are experts in this department in the Survey Company of the Royal Engineers, we had to make our own maps as we went along or accept one of the two alternatives of relying upon the old inaccurate maps supplied or going without.

One night, upon being summoned to the Colonel's tent, I was instructed to report to Divisional Headquarters in response to an order for the attendance there of a " mapper." Armed with light revolver equipment, I accordingly set out upon the two-mile walk back to Enab, where the Divisional staff occupied a large house on the highest point in the village. Upon arrival, I was ushered into the presence of a highly placed Staff Officer who, upon my presenting my credentials, received me with a courtesy and grace of manner he would usually accord to one of his own rank.   He was engaged in studying a number of maps opened out upon a table, the sight of which immediately conveyed to me the subject of the interview.   He commenced by saying that the field sketches which we had executed had come to his notice, and had been of great assistance to the General and himself in the planning of the future operations.   We were doing valuable work, and he wished to tender his own personal thanks.   He then turned to a map of the district, referred to several landmarks, and intimated that he wanted a sketch made of a certain section of the enemy's line as viewed from the ruins of Kustul, which dominated the positions in question.   Could I do it?   I jumped at the opportunity and answered that I could, whereupon he gave me further particulars and instructions to make the sketch the following day and bring it to him at night.

Laden with sketching materials, compass, fieldglasses and rangefinder, and armed with a revolver, I made my way the next morning to the isolated knoll upon which the ruins of Kustul are visible from a great distance around.   This was actually in front of the outpost line and equally under observation by the Turks, as were their trenches from that eminence. Great care was therefore necessary in order to avoid detection by their artillery, which would have rendered the place untenable.

I hid myself amongst the fallen masonry of a ruined house, and through the glasses subjected the landscape to a scrutiny such as it surely had never before experienced.   The view obtained from Kustul towards Jerusalem is very extensive, commanding the valley of Kolonia or Wady Beit Hannina and the opposite ridge.   To the extreme right, nestling amongst olive groves and terraced vineyards, is the village of Ain

Karim where Zacharias had his summer residence, and where St. John the Baptist is supposed to have been born. There are many theories connecting Aim Karim with events in Biblical history, though their authenticity seems to be somewhat mixed. Most of them, however, originated during the Crusading periods.

The village lies in a hollow, and was at this time in " No Man's Land," for the Turks had constructed their defences upon the higher ground to the north and east. Carrying the eye farther round across the broad deep valley of Kolonia, the enemy's works were easily traceable following the line of the ridge, and movement could be distinctly observed here and there, denoting the positions of his posts. To the left, stretches of the white road to Jerusalem came into view to the point where it disappeared over the distant sky-line. Again, to the left across the road were more enemy works, and the view extended round to the north-west as far as Khurbet el Burj, a hill on the summit of which stands a long rectangular building, at which point it becomes obscured by an intervening spur. This last section would be attacked by the right flank of the 74th Division in the forthcoming operations, and was that which I had to commit to paper.

I sketched assiduously until the landscape fairly shrank beneath my searching gaze. If the Turks whom I saw moving about, thereby giving me much valuable information, only knew what was going on among those ruins of Kustul—well, all would not have been so quiet and peaceful.

The sketch finished and identifying points co-ordinated from the map, I returned to camp and proceeded thence to Divisional Headquarters with the result. I was immediately admitted to the presence of the Staff Officer whom I had seen the previous night. The sketch was minutely examined, reconciled with the official maps, and pronounced satisfactory. Upon my leaving he insisted on shaking hands with me and reiterated the thanks and appreciation he had expressed at our previous interview. Orders were given for a motor-car to be got ready to drive me back to the Battalion, and as I passed out I could *feel* the stare of curiosity directed at me by a group of junior officers who lounged about the hall. As I was rushed through the cool, dark night, along the winding Jerusalem road, I felt gratified at having been able to render such service to my own and other Divisions.

Three of us had been engaged upon the panoramic sketches, and the following day we each received a letter signed by the General's " right-hand man " couched in the terms verbally expressed to me, and adding that we could rest assured that our contribution towards the success of future operations (the capture of Jerusalem) had been considerable. I still have my letter which I shall always cherish.

Whilst our Division was trekking over the plains of Philistia, the men of the 75th Division, in line with the general advance, fought their way through the Judean Hills and consolidated the line from Soba to a hill just west of Neby Samwil. It has been claimed that the 75th Division virtually captured the Holy City. True, they had accomplished a very difficult task in driving the Turks through the rugged hills, but the city was far from captured when our Division relieved them in the line before indicated, as will shortly be seen.

Neby Samwil, the ancient Mispeh and, as its modern name denotes, the traditional burial-place of the prophet Samuel, is perched on the summit of a high and conspicuous pinnacle with very steep slopes, affording one of the finest view points in Palestine. It was from the top of Neby Samwil that the Crusaders first gazed upon Jerusalem, and King Richard, covering his eyes, cried out " Ah, Lord God! I pray that I may never see thy Holy City, if I may not rescue it from Thine enemies." Under the old name of Mispeh, Neby Samwil was the scene of many outstanding events in the wars of the Israelites under Samuel against the Philistines in the former's great struggle for freedom, and of the choosing of Saul as the first King of Israel. When we were established before the Jerusalem defences the Turks occupied the knoll which, being an excellent natural stronghold, formed a very formidable obstacle to our further progress. The height of Neby Samwil had to be taken before the contemplated general attack could be embarked upon, and the task was allotted to the 180th Brigade. The Turks fought desperately to retain their hold upon the hill, but our troops stormed it again and again, until at length they dislodged the enemy at the point of the bayonet, and consolidated the position.

On the top of Neby Samwil stood a minaret that was added by the Saracens to a Crusader's Church, and was famous among tourists and pilgrims for affording a magnificent view of the surrounding country in general and of the Holy City in particular. After the Turks had been driven from this ostensibly impregnable stronghold, they began to shell it intermittently for several days. One shell hit the minaret fair and square, and it distributed itself amid the other debris lying around. Some of the shells, fired at too great an elevation, burst in the village of Beit Nakuba, on the hill slope behind our camp. A native woman was killed on one such occasion, the fact being brought to our notice by a great noise of wailing set up by her relatives, which they continued until sundown.

It should be distinctly understood that Palestine does not enjoy the perpetual sunshine which the popular though mistaken idea would suggest. From about April to the middle of November, the weather does really fulfil tradition, with month after month of blue, cloudless skies and brilliant warm sunshine. The months of April and May are by far the best, for then the hillsides and wady-beds are splashed with brilliant floral colours and the joy of living is manifested by the young spring life that abounds everywhere. Before the summer is half over, the sun has dried up all vegetation, leaving the country parched and barren with nothing but the everlasting olive tree to relieve the monotony of the stony hills. By December, winter has arrived with great banks of leaden clouds which come rolling over the hill-tops, and wind, rain and cold hold sway over the land for three or four months. It was weather such as this that we were experiencing when, on December 7th, 1917, we struck camp, dumped packs and bivouacking paraphernalia and, equipped in "battle order," commenced the steep climb to the village of Soba, in the pouring rain, to capture the Holy City.

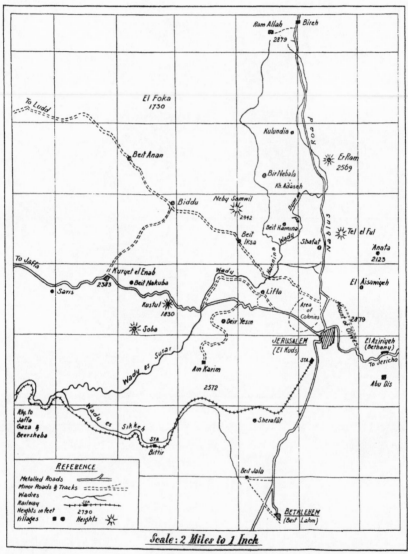

THE ADVANCE ON JERUSALEM.

CHAPTER XIII

THE CAPTURE OF JERUSALEM (*December 7th, 9th,* 1917)

THE hills of Palestine are extremely stony, and chiefly composed of masses of solid rock. The pathways leading to the villages (the majority of which are perched on the tops of hills) are naturally paved with white limestone, worn smooth by the tread of bare feet through the centuries. We still retained our transport camels, and in the mountainous district where the ground is covered with sharp flints, they were sadly out of their element. It was painful to see the wretched creatures struggling up the steep slopes in the driving rain, endeavouring to maintain a firm foothold on the wet, slippery stone. Sometimes, one of the camels would lose its footing and, bravely but in vain trying to recover itself, would go hurtling with its load down the hillside. Several such incidents occurred as we were climbing towards Soba, in some cases resulting in the camels' legs being broken, when there was no alternative but to shoot the poor beasts.

We assembled on a small plateau below, and to the west of the village, to await nightfall. In spite of the heavy rain our cooks lighted big fires and made tea, which helped to ameliorate the miserable conditions. Many men sought out large caves, which abound in the hills, and crowded together inside to shelter from the stormy weather without.

A Company of Pioneers had started in the afternoon to clear a pathway over the route we were to follow, posting men at intervals to act as guides. Without this precaution it would have been impossible to negotiate the steep and rugged country and not meet with disaster.

At eight o'clock that evening we set out upon what proved to be the most sensational achievement during the whole of the late war. Thoroughly wet and cold, we welcomed any activities to occupy the mind and tune up the circulation. To the south-east of Ain Karim, and half-way up the hill-slope on that side of the village, stands a stone watch-tower. This was our point of deployment, and we were due to arrive there at four o'clock the next morning. Eight hours seemed a superfluous allowance of time in which to get into position, and rather suggested a long dreary wait at the other end, but with strange and difficult country to negotiate in the darkness it proved to be no extravagant estimate.

Owing to the necessary caution with which we proceeded, it was not long before we evolved into single file, and stumbling over rocks and boulders, down precipitous slopes, round sheltered re-entrants and over rugged spurs, we reached the broad Wady Kolonia. Every now and then, and by a great effort, the moon fought its way through the heavy clouds and illuminated our path. After passing through many well-kept vineyards and olive groves, and rounding a rocky eminence, Ain Karim came into view through the pale moonlight, so peaceful amid the stately cypress trees which adorn the valley and lend it so much beauty, that it was very difficult to imagine that before the dawn of another day the echoes of battle would resound among its square, white houses. Very

A RATION CONVOY WINDING THROUGH THE
JUDEAN HILLS.

soon, however, the moon was again obscured by a cloud bank, and the rain continued to pour down upon us.

After all, perhaps the adverse weather conditions were really in our favour. It was a wretched night in which to move forward over strange ground to attack, and most probably the Turks considered that they would not be disturbed whilst the bad weather lasted; but, by carrying into effect the reversal of a logical conclusion, an advantage may often be gained over an opponent. So it happened on this night. A strong patrol of the 13th (London) Battalion had gone forward to capture certain Turkish outposts, and we soon met them returning with the prisoners, having accomplished their task swiftly and silently without raising an alarm.

As we were ascending the slope leading to the watch-tower, creeping alongside a low wall, the enemy, by this time alive to the fact that all was not in order, commenced to fire rapidly. Instinctively everybody crouched to the ground for cover, and there we lay for half an hour whilst the bullets pattered against the other side of the wall and sang overhead. During a lull we reached the sheltered precincts of the tower, where the Companies deployed, and proceeded round the deep re-entrant to attack the Turkish positions.

By this time the dawn had arrived, and as the enemy saw us advancing round the hill they opened a hot fire with rifles and machine guns. Men fell here and there, but the mass pushed slowly and methodically on to the objective. Presently we came under observation by a commanding spur away to the right, which was strongly held by several machine guns, which also immediately opened fire. Just as the situation was becoming critical, a third source of danger presented itself.   Suddenly, without the slightest warning, more machine guns started to fire from the ostensibly peaceful village in the rear.   For a few moments it seemed as though we were hopelessly entrapped, for, besides advancing in the face of a hail of lead, our right flank and rear were equally exposed. Bullets struck the ground all round our feet, travelling up and down our ranks, and whistling past our ears. The man on my left was shot in the stomach simultaneously with the man on my right being hit in the thigh.   By some unaccountable act of Providence I escaped unhurt.   The stretcher-bearers were busy everywhere.

The attacking Companies, now very much reduced in numbers, pushed on up the steep slope, climbed the stony terraces, and reached the line of sangars behind which the Turks were ensconced.   They continued to fire at us until the very last moment, when, seeing that escape was impossible, they offered to surrender. The sight of the recumbent and bleeding forms of our comrades lying around did not tend to promote feelings of mercy, and the tactics of the Turks had so incensed us that bayonets got to work slick and sure.   Turks who had been doing their utmost to mow us down were now on their bended knees; angry oaths were uttered, and cries for mercy rose above the din; but no quarter was given; a few bayonet thrusts, a few shots fired point-blank, and they toppled over dead.

At this juncture a Company of the 13th Battalion swept over the ridge on our right, and, after repeated bayonet charges, cleared it of the Turks whose machine guns had given us so much trouble.   At the same time the guns in Ain Karim ceased their rattling. We afterwards learned that at dawn, when the firing commenced and our attention was concentrated in the opposite direction, some Turks had kept up a sweeping fire on us, until the timely arrival of British troops speedily put a stop to their activities.

The first line of sangars was passed, and those left of the Turkish garrison were hurriedly retreating to the south-east. Our further progress was hindered, however, by the enfilade fire of a couple of machine guns to the right, secluded among the piles of stones that were dotted about, the actual position of which had not as yet been located. The whole Battalion was consequently held up. Corporal (afterwards Sergeant) Train, quickly comprehending the position, and having detected the sangar from behind which the guns were being fired, armed himself with rifle grenades, and, entirely on his own initiative, and at great personal risk, stealthily crawled round to one side and fired several of these deadly missiles with such coolness and accuracy that the whole of the two gun teams were killed. With this serious obstacle removed, the Battalion again went forward. I passed behind the sangar in question a few minutes after the event, and saw the result of the Corporal's handiwork, but the heap of mangled humanity lying there was too horrible to describe and ghastly to look upon.

For this act of bravery, which meant so much to the Battalion, Corporal Train was awarded the Victoria Cross.

The main defences of Jerusalem were now in our possession, though that holy place could not yet be considered as captured. We changed direction half left, and moved north towards the city. The ground was absolutely littered with loose stones, and in places they had been collected and piled up in large cairns, in order that the sticky red earth might be cultivated.

II

The taking of these Jerusalem defences must stand conspicuous amongst the outstanding events in the late war, as having been accomplished solely by the efforts of the infantry without the aid of artillery. Orders were issued before the attack commenced that no guns were to fire at a target within a certain radius of the Holy City, and that radius included the main Turkish positions. On the other hand, the Turks placed their batteries on the fringe of the modern suburbs, and when we gained the final ridge they fired at us unintermittently throughout the day. Their guns were only of light calibre, but were fired at zero, so that the reports of the discharges were followed immediately, almost concurrently, by the bursting of both shrapnel and concussion shells.

The 16th (London) Battalion, operating on our left along the main road, had also gained its objective, and was in line with us on the last ridge which overlooks Jerusalem from the south, across a broad valley. Our final objective that day, after capturing Jerusalem, was to have been a line drawn across the Nablus road at Tel el Ful, two miles north of the city. The plan was for the 53rd Division to advance along the Hebron road, pass Jerusalem to the east, and join forces with our Division on the Mount of Olives, with the right flank describing a protective curve across the Jericho road to Abu Dis. Thus it will be seen that such a line would have completely cut off the Holy City and protected it from the north and east—the only two directions from which the Turks could have counterattacked. Unfortunately, the 53rd Division were unable to keep to the time-table, having met with a stronger resistance than was anticipated. However, there we were, ready and waiting to go on to our final objective, with our right flank unprotected and well

in the air. Being then on the extreme right of the
British line, we had to adopt the defensive against any
likely attack from the east until the arrival of the
flank guard.

In the capacity of Battalion observer I worked my
way forward, and found seclusion in a quarry just over
the crest of the ridge. From this vantage point a most
comprehensive view was obtained; a view so teeming
with interest that it would have touched the heart of
the most stoical of observers. I then knew the sensa-
tions of the pilgrim who, with thousands of others,
travels great distances on foot and suffers untold
privations to gaze, for the first and only time, upon
the long-anticipated Zion—undoubtedly the greatest
event during the whole lives of the multitudes who
undertake the journey. There, spread out before me,
across the stony, treeless valley, was Jerusalem, the
holiest spot on earth, which had been besieged and
destroyed, rebuilt, and destroyed again and again
more times than any other city in the world. That
this much-coveted place, this jumble of buildings
ancient and modern, the scene of so much strife and
suffering throughout history, whose square, flat-roofed
houses and black-domed churches mark the positions
of many sacred spots, this city of our dreams wherein
so much has happened upon which our religion is
built, that this much-coveted place, I repeat, was now
really within our grasp, and that we would shortly
occupy it, were facts which, during our enforced wait
on those cold dreary hills, afforded much food for
contemplation. The trials and hardships which had
attended our advance from the desert country around
Beersheba sank into insignificance when considered in
the light of a price for this very great privilege of not
only gazing upon, but of having helped to capture

Jerusalem, with early prospects of treading the soil of the Holy City. I felt thankful to God for bringing me safely to this point, and imagined how much thousands of devout Crusaders of old would have given to be in a similar position.

I focused my glasses, and greedily feasted my eyes upon the wonderful sight before me. Not being then familiar with the geography of Jerusalem, I was only able to indulge in a superficial scrutiny, paying no regard to the host of minutiæ, an intimacy with which adds so much fascination to the survey of so unique a panorama. That portion of Jerusalem visible from the Enab road, and the hills on either side, chiefly consists of the modern suburbs, which extend almost to the neighbouring village of Lifta, and occupies a long spur which slopes down in a south-easterly direction to the junction of the valleys Kedron and Hinnom. At this point, just a corner of the old walled city comes into view. Almost without exception, the buildings of the modern quarter are of white stone, with red tiled roofs. Beyond the city to the north rises the conical-shaped mound, Tel el Ful, towards which we should then have been advancing. To the right continues a high ridge, comprising Mount Scopus and the Mount of Olives, on the highest point of which stands the great German hospice, with its lofty tower dominating the country in all directions. To the extreme right a stretch of about a mile of the Hebron road was visible, along which large bodies of horsemen were moving towards Jerusalem, their numbers being rapidly swelled by others hurrying in from all quarters. They were undoubtedly Turkish cavalry, and their presence there, with no signs of the 53rd Division, accounted for our inability to move forward.

Carrying my gaze across the panorama to Lifta, I discerned a continual procession of Turkish infantry, with pack mules, hurriedly coming out from Jerusalem, and concentrating in a large plantation enclosed by thick hedges. They were evidently preparing to repel an expected attack, so I watched intently for developments. I was not kept waiting long, for presently rifle and machine-gun fire came from that direction, and out of a hollow to the west emerged lines of British troops in extended order, advancing across the open country. They were subjected to heavy fire from the plantation, but that daunted them not at all. They continued to advance as coolly and apparently as unconcernedly as if engaged upon practice operations on the rolling downs of Salisbury Plain. The Turks were evidently very disconcerted at their inability to check the oncoming foe, and in a few minutes were retracing their steps as hurriedly as they had gone out to take up the defensive. Our troops reached the plantation, changed direction north, and were lost to view as they passed behind the straggling buildings of the western suburbs.

The day was well advanced, and we began to consider what arrangements could best be made for spending the night. Having spent the previous night negotiating difficult hills in the drenching rain, followed by a very strenuous day's fighting, Nature began to assert herself now that the excitement was over, and everyone felt the great need of sleep. We had neither greatcoats nor bivouac sheets, so our prospects were far from encouraging. We simply had to make the best of adverse circumstances, as we had often done before.

A thought was now given to the wounded and missing. Each platoon commander held a roll-call, and took a note of those still unaccounted for.   Small search-parties were formed, who set out to scour the hills for any wounded men not yet found by the stretcher-bearers.   It was impossible to search thoroughly the whole of the extensive area we had passed over before darkness set in, and it is to be regretted that some poor fellows, lying out wounded that night, without food or medical attention, died of their wounds, their condition being aggravated by the intense cold.

With the approach of night the sky cleared, and the landscape was illuminated by a bright moon. Notwithstanding the success which had crowned our efforts that day, we were not yet entitled to presume our position absolutely secure.   It was therefore out of the question to light fires to make tea or warm bully-beef, in order to help combat the elements. Men huddled together in small groups behind stone sangars, which they had built for warmth, and settled down in an endeavour to obtain a much-needed rest. But very little sleep came to any of us that night, owing to the bitter cold.   Half the Battalion was up running about in order to speed up the circulation, and the members of a patrol which had gone out to reconnoitre the valley between our ridge and Jerusalem were the objects of considerable envy.   Those to whom sleep came, through their being so utterly worn-out, lay shivering and moaning, whilst others passed the night in alternate half-hours of lying down to rest and running up and down a selected pitch trying to keep warm.   Ugh!   It was a wretched night.

Never was a sunrise more welcome than when, next morning, the glowing orb gradually appeared from behind Jerusalem to cheer our hearts and warm our numbed bodies.   Thus stimulated, men bustled about and gathered dried grass (which was difficult to find after the recent rains), lighted fires, and made small quantities of tea with water from their bottles, or cooked bully-beef mixed with biscuit crumbs and water, which, to us, constituted an excellent meal.

The Turks had withdrawn from Jerusalem during the night, and in the morning sent out a parliamentaire, and surrendered the city. With the arrival of the 53rd Division during the day, the advance was continued, and the line consolidated, as originally intended, across the Nablus road at Tel el Ful to the north of Jerusalem, along the ridge of Olivet, continuing across the Jericho road to the east, with the right flank resting on the hill occupied by the village of Abu Dis.

We spent the morning waiting for orders to move forward, a respite which afforded us an opportunity for scraping some of the mud from our clothing, and generally cleaning up. Some brave fellows actually shaved. At midday we moved on to the Gaza-Jerusalem road, and were there met by our ration and water convoy. The Brigade was about to march into Jerusalem, and our Battalion would lead the column.

On a ridge about a mile before the city, a Turkish guard-house stood on the left of the road. This had been the headquarters of the 16th Battalion during the attack, and, as we marched by, men of that Unit were burying their dead comrades in the adjoining garden. Just over the ridge, and alongside the road, were two Turkish field-guns, the gunners and teams of which had all been shot by the Lewis guns of the " 16th," and were still lying there as evidence of the grim struggle.

After some difficulty our pipers managed to tune up their instruments (which had suffered considerably from the recent damaging conditions), and they played us along the white road towards the western suburbs. The skirl of the pipes, accompanied by the drums, created a great sensation amongst the few Arab and Jewish pedestrians whom we passed, and, as we marched between the houses, the excitement rapidly rose to such a pitch that it was difficult to maintain a clear passage for the column. People of all ages, and apparently of all nationalities, thronged the roadway, crowded at their doors and windows, and squeezed themselves on to the roofs of their houses. Swarms of children, Arab, Jew and Christian, ran with us as we marched along, and the populace generally clambered to any point of vantage, waving and clapping their hands, cheering and singing. Jews clad in European dress came running up, singled out any one of us, wrung him by the hand, and— talking excitedly in broken English—said that they, the people of Jerusalem, had been waiting for that hour for two and a half years. Many young Jews accompanied us along the Jaffa road as we approached the city, chatted with us in the most friendly spirit, and made cigarettes for us from their own meagre stock of tobacco. The greatest enthusiasm was evinced at our arrival. Never was a welcome made more manifest than that accorded to the British troops on the occasion of the delivery of Jerusalem from the bonds of Turkish oppression.

December 9th, 1917, was, without doubt, the greatest day known to the inhabitants of Jerusalem for many weary years.

CHAPTER XIV

I⊤ soon became apparent that we were to be accommodated for the night in billets. We quitted the scene of the manifestations of exuberant joy which had been exhibited along the Jaffa road, turned down a side road, and approached a collection of large houses which, in better days, had been very attractive residences. They were substantially built of stone, though owing to prolonged neglect were then in a very dilapidated condition. Their interiors were crudely decorated, and were, in many instances, gaudy, whilst most of the windows required reglazing. The floors of the lower apartments were of coloured marble, tastefully laid out in various patterns. The general appearance of these houses would have gladdened the heart of any jobbing builder at home who had happened upon bad times. But whatever their merits or demerits, they were decidedly attractive to us, being the first houses many of us had entered for close upon six months.

It needs very little campaigning experience to render one insensible to strange surroundings and ever-changing conditions. The majority of us had not slept for three days and two nights, so we needed little inducement to depart into the land of dreams now that we were sheltered from the driving rain, and more or less protected from the wind, which moaned round the houses and through the broken windows. Also, for the time being relieved from all anxiety concerning the military situation, little or no heed was paid to the guns that roared out during the night from the positions they had that evening taken up to the north of the town.

The next day our transport and baggage arrived, and in the afternoon we left Jerusalem to take our place again in the line. A relief was effected with the 74th Division in the sector on either side of the Nablus road, our Battalion occupying the hills immediately north of the village of Shafat (the City of Nod). The Turks in this sector had retired farther to the north, and with Headquarters at Bireh, the ancient Beeroth, had taken up a forward line running from El Jib and Bir Nebala, across the Nablus road to Er Ram (Ramah, the birthplace of Samuel), thence swinging round south, *via* a hill known as Ras et Tawil and Anata (the Scriptural Anathoth), to a point about a mile east of Abu Dis, south of the Jericho road.

We remained in the line until December 16th, during which time nothing of moment took place. A forward observation post was established on a hill in front of our positions, and from here much useful information was gained. Enemy troops could clearly be seen in Bireh and Ram Allah, and large bodies of them were observed moving along stretches of the main road that here and there comes into view as it pursues its winding course between the hills.

One morning, accompanied by a fellow-scout, I set out in search of water, which was required for washing purposes. Running streams are unknown in the district, and not possessing the magic power of water divining, we were confronted by the task of tracking down, by scoutcraft, any well that might exist in the neighbourhood. Several shown on the map were found to be dry or to have fallen in, so little assistance was gained from that source. We made our way up the Wady Beit Hannina, the name by which the Valley of Kolonia is generally known, as far as the village of Beit Hannina. Here we carefully scoured the clumps of olive trees growing in close proximity, and followed the many small tracks that branch off at intervals, any one of which might have led to the object of our search, but without success. The villagers most assuredly obtained water from somewhere near by, perhaps, though hardly likely, in the village itself; so to the village we repaired to investigate. It looked quite picturesque, even from a short distance away, as do all Arab villages; but as the stranger draws nearer, the ascribed reputation is found to be no exaggeration, for filth and rubbish abound everywhere to offend the sight and smell. Beit Hannina is no exception to the general rule. The village was deserted. We commenced to search for signs of a well, but again were unsuccessful. As we were about to pursue our quest farther afield our attention was suddenly arrested by the sound of harsh feminine voices shouting and screaming in great excitement a short distance away. There was no one in sight, so we made in the direction whence the noise came, and found two old Arab women and a young girl waving their arms about, wringing their hands and shrieking with much vehemence at a couple of British soldiers. Each of the men was struggling with a large wooden door painted bright blue, which he was endeavouring to carry over a loosely constructed stone wall. The natives were evidently the first to return to the village after the recent fighting, during which the population had gone to some neighbouring caves for safety. Wooden doors, especially bright blue ones, are indeed a rare embellishment in an Arab village, so the protestations to which the natives gave voice with so much feeling upon seeing their valued property being calmly carried off by strangers, will readily be understood. The strangers, however, remained quite unperturbed. The acquisition of those doors, which they required for firewood, perhaps would mean several hot meals for themselves and comrades, so without taking the slightest notice of the shrieking women, they carried off their prizes to a camp higher up the wady. Of course, the incident had nothing whatever to do with us, and we were not there to administer justice. We were out searching for water, and by some means or other meant to find it. Thinking that the natives would assist us, we approached them and inquiringly uttered the word " moya " (water). (I could not help recalling the occasion at Sheria when the Turkish prisoners uttered that same word to us.) The women evidently thought we were looking for more blue doors. They certainly misconstrued our intentions, and immediately indulged in a great display of arm waving, shouting and raving, just as they had done towards the two miscreants then making themselves scarce up the wady. We did not like the unpleasant light in the ladies' eyes, so deemed it prudent to retire modestly, leaving them to make the best of their misfortune.

Before finally leaving the village we availed ourselves of the opportunity of inspecting a large tomb or " holy place " which stood on the outskirts. One or more of these structures may be seen in

practically every village in the country. They
have been compared with the "high places" so
often mentioned in the Bible. They are called
"makoams," and, according to tradition, mark the
site of some holy spot, or the burial-place of a saint
or religious Sheikh to whom they are dedicated.[1]
More often than not they are merely the outcome of a
piece of deception practised long ago by a local Sheikh
or Elder, to provide a source of income to himself
from his ignorant followers. Usually, the office of
the "makoam" is to keep away evil spirits, ward
off sickness, and generally to provide a "place"
where the people can appeal for help to the particular
prophet or saint who is supposed to be in attendance
every Friday. The benefit obtained varies, of course,
according to the amount paid to the custodian. In
the event of a death the corpse is placed inside the
tomb to be delivered of all influence from the Evil
One, and little earthenware lamps resembling saucers
with the edges curled up, are filled with oil and left
burning day and night. All this clearly goes to
demonstrate the superstition in which the fellaheen
are bound up.

We entered the "makoam," which was a circular
building not more than twelve feet in diameter, about
eight feet from floor to ceiling, and with a dome-
shaped roof. The place was quite devoid of
furniture, and on one side of the door was an empty
coffin with straight sides, crudely made of unplaned
wood. On the floor beside the coffin stood an
earthenware pot which had once contained oil, and
in a niche in the wall were a number of these small

---

[1] Some of the "holy places" or "makoams" in Palestine are
credited by Christians, Moslems, and Jews alike, an example of
one of these being Rachel's Tomb near Bethlehem.

lamps, blackened with age and long usage, and a matchbox bearing the name of a well-known brand of matches, but empty. Our feelings in the silent tomb-house, intensified by the presence of the empty coffin, were decidedly eerie, so we hastily took our leave and continued our search for water, an apparently fruitless errand. We eventually alighted upon a well of discoloured water, quite close to our camp—almost on our doorstep, which was found to be sufficient for our needs, though pronounced by the experts as unfit for drinking.

On the appointed day we were relieved by the 180th Brigade, and returned to Jerusalem for a ten days' rest. Ten whole days out of the line to be spent in this wonderful town seemed too good to be true; yet it was so. We went into billets near the British Agricultural Institute, which is situated in the north-western suburbs among the Jewish Colonies.

So many excellent works on the Holy City and its history have been compiled by eminent theologians and travellers, that I will defer to their much abler pens. Some impressions of the Jerusalem of to-day and its people, however, conceived by those who captured the place, may be of interest to the reader.

Jerusalem is divided into two distinct parts, the old walled city, and the extensive modern suburbs, which again are subdivided into colonies, where the people of each nationality form little communities among themselves. Estimates of the number of the population vary from fifty thousand to sixty thousand, more than half of which is composed of Jews, and these can in turn be divided into about six sections. Among the Christians the followers of the Greek Church predominate; then come the Latins, Armenians, Syrians, Copts, and lastly, the

Protestants. The latter, though small in numbers, have been instrumental in relieving a great deal of distress among the Jews and Christians. With the exception of the churches, practically every building worthy of the name is either a monastery or convent, hospital, school or other institution endowed and maintained by foreign charity, without which the poverty-stricken population could not exist. Of industries there appear to be none beyond the production of everyday commodities in quantities barely sufficient for the needs of the inhabitants. Flocks of sheep and goats may be seen scrambling over the neighbouring hills in search of pastures, attended by a shepherd, who, from appearances, is an exact replica of his forefathers of Biblical times, but the barren nature of the country, devoid of verdure in any appreciable quantity, prevents the development even of pastoral pursuits.

In normal times Jerusalem depended in a very large measure upon the yearly influx of visitors from Europe and America, but during the war, when that source of income ceased, the people were reduced to abject poverty, a condition towards which an apathetic Government remained apathetic and attempted in no way to relieve; in fact, the Turks commandeered what meagre supplies there were, apportioning a very inadequate allowance for the needs of the people. Then again, to add to the general misery, the Turks endeavoured by every subterfuge and device to press the citizens into their army, and it was with the utmost difficulty in many cases that these designs were frustrated. Numbers were forced to submit. I spoke to one woman whose husband, an Armenian, was compelled to serve in the Turkish Army. He deserted, was caught again, and finally lost his life in the fighting around Gaza. Such tyranny can only embitter the people, and breed a hatred against the Turks which they could never hope to dispel. The wild jubilation exhibited at our arrival, therefore, obviously needs no explanation.

At the commencement of the British occupation, an atmosphere of depression and want pervaded the whole town. Half the shops were closed; those that kept their doors open had only old stock to sell, composed for the greater part of gaudy, cheap souvenirs. The people one passed in the streets had poverty and hunger stamped across their pinched faces, whilst their clothes, even among the better classes, were mended and adapted, and could not be better described than as " shabby genteel." All this is chiefly applicable to the Jews. The Arabs and Yemenites (Arab-Jews), owing to their different mode of life, are very much hardier, and did not appear to be so affected by such adversities, though any signs of emaciation that existed were concealed beneath their flowing robes.

The roads in and around Jerusalem were found to be in that state of neglect and dilapidation which is so characteristic of Turkish rule, and one of the first tasks undertaken by the British was to repair them with the abundance of material to be found locally. In this work employment was given to all the poor people who wanted it. Hundreds of Jews and Arabs, men, women and children, were engaged for five piastres per diem, and many were the pathetic sights to be witnessed among these road-mending parties. The respectable citizen, down-at-heel, but still dignified, laboured side by side with the ragged vagabond. An elderly Jew, intelligent-looking and without doubt a gentleman, bareheaded, dressed in a faded frock-coat cut to the style of twenty years ago, with woollen gloves upon his hands, would be shovelling stones from a heap into a basket. His equally respectable wife, who, clad in a brilliant-coloured petticoat—purchased, maybe, at some cheap bazaar—and with a handkerchief covering her grey hair, would carry the basket of stones farther along, where they were scattered evenly over the needy road. Little Jewish girls, scantily dressed in cotton frocks and with holes in the stockings that encased their skinny legs, struggled along with smaller baskets of stones, whilst the younger and stronger men of the party either loosened the surface with picks or added to the heaps of stones from the supply in the immediate neighbourhood.

I have often tried to account for the presence of such vast quantities of stones and boulders that are scattered over the hills of Palestine. Of course, it might be said that they are the direct result of the shower of stones which Jehovah caused to rain upon the confederated Canaanites around Gibeon when they were being pursued by Joshua. Doubtless, though, a more likely explanation is that they owe their existence to the natural crumbling, for countless ages, of the great masses of solid rock of which the Palestine hills are chiefly composed. However this may be, they were a very valuable acquisition in the road repairing task then in hand, were easily accessible, and called for no transport beyond the few yards to the scene of operations.

Local resources with regard to supplies, labour and accommodation were requisitioned, and administrative machinery set up and at once put in motion to provide meals for the necessitous inhabitants. The large block of buildings in the centre of the town

I

which comprised the Russian hospital, and which had been utilized by the Turks to house their own sick and wounded, fell into our hands complete with patients and nursing staff.   The latter were despatched " down the line " to the stationary hospitals, and the buildings and medical equipment taken possession of by our own Field Ambulances. The improved facilities thus provided were indeed a boon to the Medical Corps, who had hitherto been carrying on their valuable work under very difficult conditions, and the serious cases were at last given a chance to recover sufficiently to enable them to withstand the long and hazardous journey to the Base hospitals.

Soon after our arrival, the general state of decay and stagnation which was everywhere in evidence rapidly began to disappear.   Shops which had been shut since the beginning of the war opened again; people went about their daily tasks brightly and with light hearts, and altogether the place assumed an atmosphere of cheerfulness and activity.   The Jews —be it said to their credit—were quick to perceive the most likely channels in which their natural business propensities could be turned to advantage, both to themselves and to us.   Needless to say, after many months of hard campaigning on bully-beef and biscuits, soldiers feel the need of a change of diet, and experience a longing for those delicacies which they have had to do without.   It was not long before nearly every shop, and a large percentage of the private houses, were ready to supply our wants in the shape of teas, and, in some instances, dinners, too, the principal item in the latter being goat flesh.   The favourite article of confection was what the men soon termed " fig roll."   This was made of wholemeal dough rolled out thinly and spread with minced figs, which was then rolled up tightly and baked in lengths varying from twelve to eighteen inches.

Hitherto the currency of the Ottoman Empire had, of course, been in vogue in Palestine, and the Egyptian money with which we were paid was practically unknown to the inhabitants. Upon our presenting Egyptian notes to a shopkeeper in payment for a purchase they were at first viewed askance, until an assurance was given by the authorities of their validity and worth. We, on our part, refused to accept Turkish money as change, except at a considerable and authorized discount. It is clear, therefore, that the limited stock of coin distributed amongst so many by the shopkeepers and others soon became exhausted, and as our Field Cashier came prepared with notes only, a situation presenting some difficulty was created. Upon tendering an Egyptian fifty-piastre note in payment for purchases amounting to, say, thirty piastres, the following would be handed out as change :

Four or five Turkish nickel coins worth about two piastres each,

A number of very large discs bent hollow, pierced with holes and covered with strange hieroglyphics,

About a dozen minute coins of various sizes and metals that might have been in use when Joseph's brethren bought corn in Egypt and

A handful of almond nuts to make up the amount; a most unsatisfactory state of affairs !

It was usually impossible to check the value of so mixed a collection of coins, and rather than go to any trouble in the matter the majority of men accepted them for what they were worth, knowing full well that they, in turn, would pass them on in some future transaction. This miscellaneous supply of small change soon gave out, and upon entering the shops intending purchasers were apprised of the fact, before business commenced, that " no change " was available : a circumstance which generally meant spending fifty piastres on all kinds of things you did not want in order to obtain that upon which you had set your heart. The more avaricious Jews, true to inborn tendencies, took advantage of the position, and raised their prices to an extent amounting to gross imposition. Naturally, this was strongly resented by the troops. A story quickly went round of how two Australians retaliated by a trick upon a particularly greedy shop-keeper. One of them entered the shop, leaving the other outside. Several purchases were made, amounting to a round sum, and the purchaser extracted from a wallet what appeared to be, to all intents and purposes, a brand new note carefully folded in four. The shopkeeper picked it up with an expression on his face of grave apprehension. Never in his life before had he seen paper money of this particular make; so, always on the safe side, he rejected it with the remark, " Ah! no good, no good! " At this the intrepid warrior affected great surprise, not to say indignation. He assured the Jew that the " note " was quite good, and to prove his veracity called in a passer-by—his friend—to confirm his statement. Meanwhile, the Jew gabbled away excitedly in a mixture of Yiddish and Arabic. The position was explained to the newcomer, who picked up the object of suspicion, turned it over, and pointing to the facsimile of the signature of a certain

jam manufacturer printed thereon, pronounced the
" note " to be " Good, British, new." Partly
reassured, and remembering, maybe, a similar
experience with Egyptian notes, the Jew yielded, and
accepted the jam label in payment for the goods
supplied. Later, upon realizing that he had been
" done," he lost no time in complaining bitterly to
the military authorities of the fraud that had been
perpetrated upon him. After this the situation was
improved by the importation of a large quantity of
silver and nickel coins from Egypt, which were
speedily put into circulation.

Owing to the great demand of the soldiery for
bread and cakes, the stock of flour in Jerusalem soon
sank to a dangerous ebb. In view of this, the buying
or selling of anything made of flour was strictly
prohibited by the military Governor. But where you
have a willing vendor and a willing purchaser, it is
difficult to prevent a transaction, especially when to
the one it means soft new bread for breakfast instead of
hard biscuits. In spite of explicit orders to the
contrary, men surreptitiously bought bread, etc., just
as before, and slunk back to their billets with a guilty
look on their faces and conspicuous bumps in the region
of their tunics, or a yard or so of " fig roll " concealed
up their sleeves. A length of this contraband so
concealed rendered it rather awkward to pay the
respect due to the King's Commission, and it was
generally found more convenient, in such a predicament, to engage one's attention in the opposite
direction. (This was before the abolition of the left
hand salute.)

CHAPTER XV

THE HOLY CITY

It should be remembered that Jerusalem is " the Holy City " alike to Jews, Moslems and Christians. The fundamental principles of the theocracy are accepted by all three, the coming of Christ, and the later upstart of Mohammed marking the departure of the two former from the common faith.   The Moslems, whilst rejecting the tenet that Jesus Christ is the Son of God, accept Him upon a level with their other great prophets and Apostles, namely, Adam, Noah, Abraham and Moses, and claim Mohammed to be the last and greatest of all.   The loss of Jerusalem, therefore, must have been a great moral blow to the Turks, and we afterwards learned from the inhabitants that as soon as it became apparent the city was in imminent danger the Germans attached to the Turkish force endeavoured to persuade them to retire forthwith. The Turks refused to quit their Holy City without putting up a fight in its defence, so the Germans went alone, leaving their allies to bear the brunt of our attack.   There may be something to be said for the Germans' decision not to resist their co-religionists on ground held sacred by both, but such a position is one of the results always to be expected of an allegiance in arms between peoples whose religions are diametrically opposed, a union which, in times of adversity, can only lead to a split in their forces. Had the Germans remained, however, there are no grounds for supposing that the result of the operation would have been different.

Immediately upon our occupation of Jerusalem a state of Martial Law was proclaimed, and our Commander, General Allenby, with characteristic good taste, put all Moslem places of worship under Moslem military control. The Church of the Holy Sepulchre was placed under a British Guard, and sentries were stationed at the gates of the city, which was placed out of bounds to the troops. Later, much to our satisfaction, permission was given for the arrangement of parties to visit the old city, and I lost no time in attaching myself to one of these.

There are six gates to Jerusalem in use to-day, i.e., the Damascus Gate and Herod's Gate on the north, St. Stephen's Gate on the east, Dung Gate and Zion or David's Gate on the south, and the Jaffa Gate on the western side. A very old Moslem tradition says that when the Christians take Jerusalem the conqueror will make a triumphal entry by the Golden Gate, which is on the eastern wall, and no doubt this belief accounts for it having been walled up for so long. The tradition has now been doubly disproved, for on December 11th General Allenby entered by the Jaffa Gate, and on foot, with a total absence of the pomp and triumph which has for centuries been predicted.

The Jaffa Gate is at the foot of Jaffa Street, the main thoroughfare outside the walls, and is the principal entrance. Perhaps, though, it is incorrect to say that the actual gate is in use at all, for it has been superseded by an opening made in the wall, and was closed at the time of which I write. In 1898 the Ex-Emperor of Germany visited Jerusalem, and as none but a conqueror may drive through the gates, a portion of the wall was knocked down to allow that personage to pass through in his customary manner— one of the greatest pieces of vandalism imaginable. Poised on the wall overlooking the opening, is a clock-tower of white stone erected, it is presumed, by way of recompense. Now, as a clock-tower, there is nothing to be said against it, and it would no doubt look quite well adorning a public building in a European City; but standing as it does in a setting of such glorious antiquity, it appears positively hideous and shrieks at the passer-by, calling attention to the incongruity of its prominent position.

The walls of Jerusalem are very massive, and appear to be built upon a sub-structure, sinking in places to a depth of about thirty feet. Notwithstanding that you are sorely tempted to imagine that the Jerusalem of to-day is the same city that Christ knew, it is, nevertheless, comparatively modern, the walls dating back only to 1539-42, when they were reconstructed by Sultan Suleiman. The only portion remaining of the city destroyed by Titus in A.D. 70 is the Tower of David, which is a portion of the Citadel preserved by that General to provide shelter for his soldiers, and which Josephus calls the "Tower of Phasaelus." Any other remains that may exist lie buried more than thirty feet below the street level, from which the conclusion may be drawn that the practice during the long period of intermittent destruction the city has suffered was to build each new city upon the ruins of its predecessor.

After passing through the breach in the wall which serves as the Jaffa Gate, you proceed along a narrow street which is crowded with people dressed in all manner of Eastern and semi-Eastern costumes, and

rub shoulders with swarthy Arabs, hungry-looking
Jews, jet-black negroes, thick-set bearded Russians,
and stately Bedouins, all busily engaged upon their
various daily pursuits. The male members of one sect
of Jews, who always look wretchedly poor, wear long
cork-screw curls in front of the ears, and the majority
of them, if seen walking about in Chelsea or the Latin
Quarter of Paris, would immediately pass for Christ
models. The poky little shops on either side seem to
occupy archways in the stone walls, and the vendors
either transact business sitting cross-legged among
their wares, or lounge against the crazy wooden door-
posts gossiping with neighbours. Presently, the
street becomes so narrow that it is difficult to make
headway through the motley throng. An Arab
pushes by you, leading a diminutive donkey which
clatters over the uneven cobble-stones, almost
completely hidden beneath a prodigious load, and
stepping on one side to allow the beast to pass, you
come into sudden and unexpected contact with the
wet and shining goat skin of a water carrier. A little
farther on, the closely packed houses meet overhead,
and the street continues beneath a tunnel, the
buildings forming the roof. The light is so subdued
that at first the unaccustomed gloom renders it difficult
to distinguish objects on either hand. The red glow
of a metal-worker's fire throws a ruddy beam of light
across the pathway, and prevents you from stumbling
over a couple of goats that are tied to a post by the
wayside. Suddenly the path emerges again into the
bright sunlight, amid a scene brilliant with coloured
robes, red tarbooshes and snowy-white turbans.
The jabber in many languages, combined with the
hustling and jostling of the continual stream of
people, is quite bewildering. So, leaving the citizens

to their buying and selling, you are glad to seek out the quieter thoroughfares in order to appreciate better that you are really treading the streets of the Holy City.

It is advisable to forget, if possible, that you have a sense of smell, otherwise the odours that emanate from every nook and corner will prove very obnoxious, for there appears to be a total absence of sanitary arrangements.

The street gradually descends by broad steps to cross the gully formed by the Tyropean Valley as it cuts its channel right through the city and, passing through an archway guarded by two massive iron-bound doors, leads to the Haram esh Sherif.   This is the name given to the large enclosure wherein stood the Temples containing the Ark of the Covenant.   It has an area of thirty-five acres and the approximate centre, where the Dome of the Rock now stands, was the summit of Mount Moriah, though by the levelling down from time to time of the mass of debris of the destroyed cities, the surface is quite flat.   Sir Charles Wilson truly described the surrounding buildings as " the finest mural masonry in the world, capable, even in its decay, of affecting men's minds more strongly than any other buildings of the ancient world."   On the northern side, bordering on the Mohammedan quarter of the city, is a glorious pile of buildings gradually crumbling away, with tiny square windows dotted over the outer walls and mysterious barricaded doorways inviting one's speculations as to where they lead.   These buildings were formerly used as Turkish barracks.

The Dome of the Rock, or Mosque of Omar, is a magnificent octagonal building externally decorated with tiles of various colours, into which

verses of the Koran are worked in blue and white.
The structure is surmounted by a large black dome
of wood, which was repaired by Saladin. According
to tradition, the site occupied by the mosque was
where Abraham prepared to offer up Isaac, where
Jacob saw the ladder leading towards heaven, and
where stood Solomon's Temple containing the Ark,
and the great sacred rock within the mosque is said to
be that by which Mohammed prayed, and then
ascended heavenward upon his mysterious steed, El
Burak. As one writer says, " Here was the centre of
the religious, the poetical, and the political life of God's
chosen nation. And then one thinks of the defeats
and disasters consequent upon disobedience; how glory
after glory vanished, until alien powers desolated and
utterly destroyed the holy place. One thinks of
devout Jews in every land, oppressed and burdened,
turning towards the sacred site, and remembering it
with tears as they pray for restoration to their land."
Volumes can be, and have been, written upon the
Haram esh Sherif alone. A discourse upon its
history, however, would be outside the province of
this narrative, and I could not attempt to do the
subject anything approaching justice without repeating
what has already been written by eminent authorities.

It is not necessary to possess an imagination
beyond the average in order to picture this great
enclosure at the time of its splendour, three thousand
years ago. Solomon built his wonderful Temple,
according to plans handed him by David, on the very
spot, we are told, where the Dome of the Rock now
stands, and sat " in all his glory " to pronounce his
judicial decisions and receive Princes from foreign
kingdoms who came to pay tribute to the profound
sagacity with which he was endowed. The Queen of

Sheba, according to Moslem tradition, travelled all the way from Abyssinia, attended by a splendid retinue, and presented Solomon with two pillars, which are supposed to be the free standing columns now in the interior of the Golden Gate. All this, and much more, comes rushing through the mind of the onlooker, and one can almost see a gorgeous *cortège* mounting the broad stone steps on to the platform and passing through the arcaded approach to the King's throne. Portions of similar arcades are still standing, though they date no earlier than the sixth century A.D. Some four hundred years after Solomon, by way of judgment upon the Israelites for their idolatry and broken faith with Jehovah, the hosts of Babylon came from east of the Jordan, pillaged the Temple and laid the place waste. Then, later still, and on the same spot, Christ dispersed the money-changers from the Temple, which they had made a den of thieves.

The eastern wall of Jerusalem is very strong and has all the appearance of a fortification. It overlooks the deep valley of Jehoshaphat, and it would be an extremely difficult undertaking, even in these days of military science, to take the city from that side by a frontal attack. By crossing the Haram esh Sherif, and mounting the ledge that gives access to the battlements, the view gained is unparalleled for its Biblical associations. The ground falls away very steeply from the base of the wall to the bed of the valley below, then rises gradually for over 300 feet to the top of the Mount of Olives, which attains an altitude of 2,765 feet above the Mediterranean. The Jericho road swings round the north-eastern corner of the wall, enters the valley, and then ascends the slope of Olivet to disappear over the sky-line in the direction of Bethany. Immediately opposite, a little

JERUSALEM TYPES.

way up the hill, is Gethsemane, and standing amid stately cypresses, is the white Russian Church of the Virgin with its five gilded domes glistening in the sun. Dominating the whole valley is the tall tower of the Russian Hospice, adding another 109 feet to the already considerable altitude of the mount upon which it stands. One of the most remarkable features of the whole scene is the great number of burial grounds in the valley and on the slopes of the Mount of Olives. They are enclosed by stone walls, and are crowded with tombstones. Right up to the city walls they are packed closely together, the oldest occupying the much-coveted position touching the wall itself. How old the graves are it is impossible to tell. Whose remains they enshrine must remain equally obscure, for no epitaphs or other markings are to be found on them; but what an honour to be buried against the wall of the Holy City!

The afternoon has now worn on to evening, and the sinking sun casts a soft warm glow over the grey city, intensifying the deep green of the cypress trees that show up in relief against the minor buildings of the enclosure. Tucked away in the north-western corner is a decrepit minaret with a wooden balcony at the top constructed of rough beams. In the midst of your reflections a clear, high-pitched voice sounds from the minaret, and standing on the balcony facing towards Mecca, with arms outstretched as though in appeal, and in a voice not unmusical, but which changes key with every other word, a priest calls all Moslems to prayer. In a minute or two the echoes of his voice die away, and as your gaze returns across the Valley of Jehoshaphat, a curious thrill passes through you upon recalling all that has happened in and around this wonderful place. The road that climbs the hill opposite must have been the route taken by the Babylonians after they had destroyed Jerusalem and carried the Jews away into captivity, and as the host disappeared over the ridge, the vanquished Israelites no doubt looked back with tearful eyes for the last time upon their city, then lying desolate and in ruins. It was somewhere on the same hill that Christ told His disciples to fetch the ass fastened near by, and, mounted thereon, He descended along that very road and entered the city by the Golden Gate, whilst the people carpeted the roads with palms.

There is so much to see, so much to think about and impress upon the memory, that your brain seems in a whirl. As you descend from the wall and recross the sacred enclosure, you are conscious of a seriousness of mind you have never before experienced. In the wildest fancies of childhood you never dreamed it was anything like this, or that you would ever walk upon the sacred soil. And even yet you have not seen one half of what Jerusalem has to offer.

Unfortunately, the limited time at our disposal for the occasion did not admit of a thorough exploration of the city, a circumstance which was generally very much regretted.

No Christian can walk along the Via Dolorosa without a feeling of profound reverence. For generations pilgrims have traversed these uneven stones in their strivings to follow the footsteps of Christ on His way to Calvary, and have dropped a tear at each of the stations where He rested or fell under the weight of the Cross. The actual street trod by Him must have been considerably below the present level, and even if the locality be true, the theory of the stations, like so many other theories, is steeped in uncertainty, for the places have been continually changed as and when convenience required. In the absence of any substantial evidence to the contrary, the tradition (for it cannot be more) that the Via Dolorosa marks the way to Calvary has gained authenticity. The site of Calvary is now generally accepted as being the one claimed for it within the Church of the Holy Sepulchre, though different authorities, from time to time, have propounded fresh theories which can but overshadow the whole subject with doubt.

Our little party reached the Church of the Holy Sepulchre only to find, to our great disappointment, that it was out of bounds to us in spite of the pass we possessed granting admittance into the city. This was the more regrettable as few of us had another opportunity of viewing the interior.

A visit to the Holy City is an experience that comes to most of us but once in a lifetime, and realizing that fact, you make every endeavour to preserve in your mind all that you have seen, for those memories will have to last you for the rest of your days. Most thinking people cannot fail to be profoundly impressed, though, incredible as it may seem, I have heard men remark upon such a visit that it was " so much waste of time." The total lack of imagination in the materialistic mind is deplorable, and a person who is incapable of appreciating the beauties and wonders of this earth, must needs excite the pity of others not so afflicted.

CHAPTER XVI

THE term of our sojourn in Jerusalem was not due to expire until after Christmas, so we were all looking forward to spending the time in surroundings so compatible with the season, and so near to the little town where the great event took place. For a week past the weather had been good, but a few days before Christmas the fine spell broke, and gave way to a cold wind and rain. A soldier out of the line always feels for his less fortunate brother who is in it, especially when the climatic conditions are such that dry skins are rare, and boots not filled with an unpleasant mixture of mud and water are things to dream about. We had every reason to congratulate ourselves upon our good fortune in enjoying the shelter of billets, and could well afford to sympathize with those who had nothing more weather-proof than bivouacs to protect them from the elements. Like all good things in the Army, this state of affairs was too good to last long, and the vagaries of war stepped in to disturb considerably our equanimity, and completely dispel our hopes for the near future. Late in the afternoon of Christmas Eve, we received orders to pack up immediately and proceed to the village of Shafat, situated in that section of the line which we had recently vacated. Extra bandoliers of ammunition

144

and bombs were issued to every man, a procedure which was viewed with much apprehension, being no part of the usual Yuletide celebrations. These sudden alarms were far too well known to us for any doubts to be entertained as to the reason. There was trouble brewing for somebody, and Christmas or no Christmas, we were going to see to it that whoever was responsible for this untimely interference with our projected festivities would be the sufferer; to wit, John Turk.

We reached Shafat and distributed ourselves among the olive trees growing to the south of the village, and there erected bivouacs in small stone wall enclosures left by another Battalion, or perhaps the Turks themselves. The horrible truth that the enemy intended to attack at midnight in a serious attempt to retake Jerusalem was then officially revealed to us. We changed our equipment into " battle order," and stood by until it should please " our friends the enemy " to commence operations. Our prospects were far from comforting, but to make matters worse the heavy skies overhead, as though in sympathy with us for our spoilt Christmas, wept copiously and long, drenching everything it was most important to keep dry, wrecking the foundations of our rock-walled habitations, and generally adding misery to our already many discomforts.

The Turks had no doubt calculated that Christmastide was most opportune to carry their plans into effect, surmising, maybe, that at such a festival we should be least prepared for such an eventuality. If so, they made a very grave mistake, as will later be seen.

The attack was expected to be made on either side of the Nablus road, and upon that sector our attention

K

and strength were chiefly concentrated. Of the Division, our Brigade was in the line, having relieved the 180th Brigade, whilst the 181st was in reserve. Two Battalions, the 13th and 16th, held the front line positions on the west and east of the road respectively, the 15th was in close support, supplying two Companies to each front line Battalion, and our Battalion was held in reserve. Though there was but one Brigade in the actual fighting line, the whole of the Divisional trench mortar batteries and machine guns went into garrison also, so that with the sixteen Lewis guns of each Battalion our positions literally bristled with armaments. Then, just behind us, were several batteries of field guns ready to put up a barrage at a minute's notice, and farther back still, heavier guns had taken up their positions. Knowing all this, one could not help harbouring a sense of security, and a feeling that the Turks could start their show as soon as ever they liked; the sooner the better, and so get the job over.

Shortly after dusk we acquired a doubtful ally in the form of a strong south-west wind, which, whilst blowing with full force in the face of the enemy, also drove the rain into our bivouacs, which were exposed to it. Nevertheless, whatever our own discomforts, a certain amount of satisfaction was derived from the thought that the lot of the Turk was even less enviable, for not only was he not so well provided against the same bad weather, but had the responsibility of carrying out a difficult task under horrible conditions.

The hours dragged along on feet of lead, and the suspense was beginning to be keenly felt. Those who had anything to smoke, smoked it; whilst others, like myself, who had not, acted according to temperament, and either passed the time cursing the wretched weather, or, seeking the seclusion of their own thoughts, conjectured as to what they would be doing on this Christmas Eve if the war had not separated them from their homes and dear ones. An issue of rum was served, which did a great deal towards counteracting the injurious effects which the wet and cold would otherwise have had upon us.

The weather was really vile, and there was still an hour and a half to wait before the reported time for the attack to commence. All was silent save for the moaning of the wind; an uncanny silence like the calm before a storm. It is bad enough to wait for the order to attack, but the suspense is very much intensified when you must count the minutes to the time when you expect someone else to attack you. Everybody was on tenterhooks when word was passed round to " stand down," for activities were no longer expected that night. If there had been no wind, I believe the Turks would have heard the great sigh of relief that escaped pretty well everyone. This piece of news seemed so absolutely authentic (such an order would never have been given had there been any shadow of a doubt), that it appeared as though the enemy, like the expected guest for whom you have been delaying dinner for an hour, had sent a telegram saying he would have to disappoint you after all.

We, accordingly, settled down to spend the rest of the night in the very best way possible under the circumstances. My companion and I had constructed a shelter by suspending our joined bivouac sheets between two low sangars built at right angles to a bank, and soon after the rain commenced, a small rivulet cut its path down the bank and through our " home." However, we ignored the intrusion, and fully dressed in overcoats and with blankets wrapped round us, we laid down in the mud and went to sleep. In spite of all, our invaluable humorists made light of our adversities, cracked seasonable jokes with one another about hanging up stockings, and inquired of the platoon Sergeant what time Santa Claus was expected. Towards morning the rain stopped, and the sudden cessation of the pattering on our roof must have awakened me. I rolled over. In so doing I, unwittingly, removed the dam which my body had effected on a pool of water, and afforded it access to my friend. He also awoke, but realizing our predicament we considered it advisable to remain perfectly still, and so obviate soaking up more water than we could help. When it became quite light I rummaged in my pack for a small volume somebody had given me in Jerusalem, and with the object of forgetting my condition began to read. The book was an account of an expedition to the South Pole, a topic more fitting for the blazing heat of the desert. The first chapter made me feel quite chilly. With the second I began to shiver; but when I came across an illustration in the middle of the third chapter of a ship picking its way through an ice-floe, I verily froze, and decided to give it up. Some men, whose bivouacs had collapsed on them during the night, were slopping about in the mud outside, so we joined them. There was mud everywhere. The clouds overhead raced along at break-neck speed, and collided with every other hill-top. The air was raw and damp. Ugh, what a morning! and Christmas morning at that!

Our heroic cooks produced fire-wood from the mysterious depths of their boxes and made tea, though the cold bully-beef and rain-sodden biscuits which constituted our breakfast completely eclipsed any comfort derived from drinking that beverage. Later in the morning we indulged in physical exercises as laid down in the text-books. If the Turks could have seen us standing with legs astride, flinging our arms heavenwards, they might have thought we were evoking the assistance of Mars, appealing to him to cause the sluices to be opened again, and so put a further damper upon their projected attack. But it was not so. We were merely trying to get warm, and in a measure were successful.

Towards midday we were given the definite assurance that the Turks would not attempt an attack until the following night at the earliest, so we moved into Shafat itself, and took possession of the native houses. To render them at all habitable it was necessary to clear out the rubbish that littered the earth floors, odd bits of native clothing, filthy straw and mud. In the afternoon the sun struggled through, and enabled us to dry some of our saturated clothing and blankets. At night all was quiet, and not having the faintest idea when we should get the next night's sleep we obtained as much rest as possible.

The next day, Boxing Day, the rain held off, and owing to the probability of the village being shelled by the Turks, we returned to our previous camping ground. In the evening the sky cleared, and with dusk a bright moon rose. Again we adopted " battle order," and were informed that the attack would be sure to take place that night. The time given was 2 a.m. All preparations were duly made. The 15th Battalion moved into its position of close support, and we supplied one Company to each of the respective Support Headquarters. One of these Companies moved to a hill called Khurbet es Soma, just to the south of Tel el Ful on the east of the Nablus-

Jerusalem road, the other occupying the hill Khurbet el Meraghib to the west of Shafat, both within easy access to, and in telephonic communication with, the unit to which they were attached. There was nothing to be done then but to wait.

As the night wore on it became very cold indeed. The moon was brilliant. At midnight rum was issued.

At two o'clock precisely on the 27th, the firing commenced, first one shot, then another and another, followed by a burst of half a dozen rounds from a Lewis gun. The echoes rolled away over the hills, and then came a brief spell of silence to be broken by several explosions of Stokes trench mortar shells, tempered by the irregular snapping of rifle fire. The battle had begun.

The field guns at our rear opened fire, putting up a fierce barrage between the advancing Turks and our positions. The gunners worked like niggers, and, notwithstanding the inclemency of the weather, several were seen in the bright flashes to be half stripped as they fed their hungry pieces. The continuous rattle of the firing in front of Tel el Ful, where the main attack was being made, and the muffled reports of bombs and trench mortars, told that the fight had swiftly developed, and was already at its height. Reports were received that the Turks had broken through, but these were not confirmed. They did actually get within a few yards of the main line trenches, but the 16th held their ground, and with the aid of the trench mortars and machine guns put up a stubborn resistance, and wrought frightful slaughter among the attackers.

The fighting raged fiercely throughout the night, and we expected any minute to be called upon to reinforce the defenders. With the coming of dawn things quieted down considerably, and during the morning there was a decided lull. Soon after midday, however, the attack was resumed with renewed vigour. Periodically, the artillery were called upon to give assistance, and then the guns spitefully belched forth their missiles in a regular tornado. Machine guns were firing incessantly. Several fresh attempts were made to break through at various points, but they were all unsuccessful. On one occasion the Turks did gain a short-lived success. After being previously repulsed they had retired to reorganize, and a certain platoon of the 16th took advantage of the respite to issue rations and snatch a hasty meal. In the middle of so doing they were surprised by the sudden appearance in their camp of a body of the enemy far outnumbering themselves. The only course open to them was to retire upon their main body. This they did, and were forced to abandon forty-eight hours' rations and several jars of rum, which the Turks promptly carried away as a great prize, which, to them, it was indeed. The ground was afterwards retaken, and the enemy were in a position no better than when they started. On the left of the road the 13th held on firmly.

Attacks had also been launched against various sections of the line held by the 53rd Division on the east, but these were no more successful than those on the north. In the evening the 53rd Division attacked. From our position the ground fell away rapidly in their direction, and we obtained an excellent bird's-eye view of the operation, including the capturing of Anata, the ancient Anathoth.

Night came again with a clear sky and brilliant moon. A suspicious silence prevailed. Of course, the force of the Turkish attack may have been spent, yet, on the other hand, they might merely have been recovering their broken strength and morale preparatory to making a further attempt. It was one of those periods of uncertainty when either might have been the case. Our Company, east of the Nablus road, was summoned to the line to relieve a company of the 16th which had suffered rather heavily during the previous twenty-four hours' fighting. In single file we traversed the steep and rocky spur of the hill behind which we had been waiting in readiness, proceeded down a deep ravine, and climbed up the opposite side to the 16th's headquarters. Here we left our packs and bivouacking paraphernalia. To proceed it was necessary to cross a piece of high ground under observation, upon which the moon was shining with what seemed to us to be excessive brilliancy. Only small parties could go across at a time, and to divert the eyes of the enemy, a gun in the rear fired at short intervals regulated by an Artillery officer by telephone to the Battery. As the shells shrieked overhead so each party made good its passage. We were conducted by guides over a piece of ploughed land, and found ourselves behind a long ridge of loose stones some six feet in height. These stones formed a capital breast-work, and lying on them were the men of the 16th keeping a vigilant look-out for any signs of activities in front. They expressed themselves very thankful to see us, the more so because the relief was unexpected. The Turks were supposed to be a hundred and fifty yards away, and it was the general opinion that they had had all the fight knocked out of them. Still, for whatever might come to pass we prepared ourselves. The relief was effected in the strictest silence not unattended by some difficulty, for the slightest movement by the men on the stones sent an avalanche rattling to the ground, creating a hair-raising noise.

Immediately before us the uneven ground was strewn with piles of stones, boulders, and dead and dying Turks. Beyond were more great piles of stones deposited from the neighbouring quarries, any one of which might have hidden a machine gun or a party of enemy riflemen. Our orders were to keep a sharp look-out and fire at anything we saw moving —orders which needed no reiteration. After a while, the strain of continual staring began to tell upon us, and we all experienced optical illusions. Notwithstanding the bright moonlight, it was difficult to identify the different objects in front, and every now and again a man, fully convinced that he saw something moving, would fire, and the complaint travelled right down the line until every man had fulfilled his duty to his conscience. I would not care to vouch that anyone really was prowling about, but if so, he was given an excellent assurance that we were ready for any contingency. And so the night wore on.

I was fully expecting to be called upon to carry out a reconnaissance of the ground in front, to learn exactly what John Turk was up to. That is one of the unenviable privileges of a Battalion Scout. It was close upon midnight, and I was discussing, in muffled whispers with my neighbour, the virtues of a drink of tea, or cocoa, or even coffee, at a time when there are no prospects of such a wish being gratified, when my name was passed from mouth to mouth along the ridge. " H'm," thought I, " the expected has happened." I carefully extricated myself from the stones I had built round me for shelter from the wind, and scrambled off the pile, my friends bestowing all manner of blessings upon my head, at the same time thanking their lucky stars that the disagreeable task was mine and not theirs. However, the work of a scout is not always disagreeable, so the rough must be taken with the smooth. Somebody had to do the job, and by chance that somebody was myself. I made my way to the Company-Commander and reported. As I have remarked in an earlier chapter, if a campaigner always sets himself to expect the worst, he is not likely to suffer any considerable disappointment. Far from disappointment, a pleasant surprise was in store for me; pleasant in one sense, but not so in another. My friend and mapping colleague at Battalion Headquarters had been wounded, and I was to return there without delay to take his place. No one in his right mind would object to being relieved from the vicissitudes of the line, but at the same time I could not refrain from wishing that the reason for my being recalled was other than it was.

It transpired, as the night wore on, that the Turks really had had all the fight knocked out of them, and nothing untoward occurred calling for special mention.

Here it would seem appropriate to pay a well-deserved tribute to our Intelligence Service. It had, undoubtedly, excelled. The initial warning on Christmas Eve, the reliable information as to the postponement of the attack, and finally, the exact time, to a minute, at which we might expect the enemy to commence operations, all clearly show to what perfection our secret agents had carried out their work, with the result that ample preparations could be made.

Perhaps it would be of interest to review shortly the operations of Christmas, 1917, as a whole. In order better to protect our lateral lines of communication along the Jaffa-Jerusalem road, and also to render those two places more secure, General Allenby had decided to advance the whole line to a depth varying from six to eight miles. The operation in the coastal sector was that first undertaken, and on December 21st and 22nd the 52nd and 54th Divisions effected a successful, though most difficult crossing of the river Nahr El Auja and, taking the enemy completely by surprise, gained their final objectives. When the time was ripe for carrying out the plans in the centre and on the right, the concentration of enemy troops around Bireh, on the Nablus road, predicted the intention of the Turks to attempt to retake the Holy City. This, as we have seen, proved to be the case. The troops employed in this operation were entirely fresh, and had escaped the demoralizing effects of our advance from the Gaza-Beersheba line; this accounts for the great determination with which the attack was made. After the initial onslaught against our positions north of Jerusalem on the 27th December, the 10th and 74th Divisions attacked in the centre, accomplishing the dual object of advancing the line, according to plan, and drawing the enemy's reserves from the Jerusalem front. Any further attempts against Jerusalem were thus prevented, and the initiative fell to us. The enemy had really played directly into our hands, for, having considerably weakened himself by throwing all his strength into the attack, we were able to carry out the plans previously made. On the 29th our Division advanced to Bireh, which was occupied in the evening, after overcoming stubborn opposition. On our left the 10th and 74th Divisions had advanced in line, whilst the 53rd Division had extended its left flank northwards to protect our right. The net result, therefore, of the Turks' only attack of any magnitude during the whole campaign was an ignominious failure, leaving him six miles farther away from his objective than when he started.

On the 31st December our Brigade marched back to Jerusalem, and we spent the night in the billets which we had left so hurriedly on Christmas Eve. The following day we took over a section of the line from the 53rd Division on either side of the Jericho road, about three miles east of the city.

CHAPTER XVII

THE scenery of Palestine has a beauty peculiar to itself. The English lakes, the snow-clad Alps, the picturesque grandeur of Italy, or the wooded mountains of Greece—to mention but a few varieties of scenery—all possess their charms, charms that enthral the spectator, and leave indelible impressions upon the memory. But in the magnificence of one or the exquisite beauty of another, we cannot find any semblance to that scenery which is the exclusive feature of Palestine. The plains of the Holy Land, unlike any others, devoid of water, bare of vegetation, and consequently without any collection of buildings of sufficient number or size to be called towns, plains that are little more than wildernesses and are sprinkled with ancient ruins that have their origin in an age when the world's history was in its infancy, plains such as these are rare. Hills? Yes, it would be difficult to find a country so flat that no particular elevation would come within that category; but a system of hills packed so tightly together that in places the intervening ravines are inaccessible, hills that are encircled by tiers of natural terraces, rich in olive groves and vineyards, and whose summits are crowned with ancient stone villages or monasteries marking ancient sites, others clothed in a mantle of loose stones and boulders, so barren that

157

nothing will grow on them—hills such as these are typical of Palestine. The flocks of black goats and long-eared sheep that eke out a meagre existence on the scanty pastures of these hills, and the figures of the Bedouin Arabs dressed in the quaint costumes of Biblical times, are inevitable in every panorama.

Palestine will affect different people in different ways, according to temperament. The hardened materialist will look upon the rolling hills of Judea, taking particular notice of the barren nature of some, and remark, " What a God-forsaken hole! " He cares not a jot for unique colouring, or the peculiar stratification of the matter composing those hills, whilst ancient villages perched on hill-tops, enveloped by an atmosphere of historic romance, or the olive groves and vineyards of fertile valleys, receive no appreciation from his short-sighted gaze. He will make jokes about the land " flowing with milk and honey," quite ignorant of the fact that in some districts, during certain times of the year, this old description is as true to-day as when it was first conceived. On the other hand, those possessing the valuable gift of knowing how to use the eyes that God gave them, make their survey with a very much wider perception. They can distinguish the various features peculiar to a particular kind of landscape, make due allowance for the geographical, historical and economic causes of those peculiar features, finding interest in that which would be wearisome to the materialist, and seeing beauty in a scene which, if viewed through less appreciative eyes, would be desolate.

Throughout the length and breadth of Palestine, "from Dan to Beersheba," there cannot be a more striking scene than that obtained from the Mount of Olives in the early morning. Whether you ascend the

Mount from the east or the west, the panorama disclosed from the summit in the opposite direction is a revelation.

.   .   .   .

During January and February the early mornings are usually very cold, and after a clear, moonlight night, a sharp frost is often in evidence. If, by chance, your way should be along the road on Olivet so early, and if time and other ruling considerations admit, it is well worth while to linger and watch the new day gradually develop. You stamp your feet on the hard road to keep them warm, and wait for the rising of the sun to sound Nature's réveillé. But all do not wait for this signal to commence the day, for climbing up the zig-zag path from the village of El Assaweiyeh is an Arab closely wrapped in his brown and white striped gibbeh—for natives though they be, the Arabs feel these cold, crisp mornings keenly.

He is driving half a dozen sheep, and following upon his heels are two of his wives dressed in customary black, carrying large bundles upon their heads, which probably contain the produce of the small cultivated patch near the village. Their destination is undoubtedly Jerusalem, in whose markets the sheep and produce will be sold. The party nearing the top of the hill are about to cross the intervening patch of ploughed land to the road. The man quickens his pace on the level, for it is very chilly, and there is an advantage to be gained in arriving at the markets early. He carries nothing but a staff, with which he prods the sheep if they show any inclination to stop and nibble at stray bits of vegetation. The women do not get along so easily as he, for the loads they carry are heavy, but their lord and master never looks round even to see if they experience any difficulty, for

to do so would be showing them that consideration
which the unalterable custom of his race forbids.   The
women catch up to him, and breathlessly reach the
road.   The party makes an interesting group, so you
arrange your perambulations to meet them at the gap
in the wall through which they will pass.   The Arab
is not a young man, for his beard is tinged with white,
and his dark skin is wrinkled and wizened by long life
in the open air.   Around his tarboosh he wears a white
turban, and his otherwise bare feet are enclosed in
stout hide shoes with turned-up pointed toes.   For
the rest of him he is covered by a thick gibbeh, which
looks more like a blanket than anything else.   He
gives you a swift, piercing glance savouring of suspicion, but immediately changing his demeanour, bids
you a cordial " syeedah," touching his brow above the
eye by way of salute, and passes on to the road leading down to the Damascus Gate.   His wives walk
barefooted, and are dressed entirely in black with
hoods over their heads.   Any natural beauty they may
have once possessed has been destroyed by disfiguring
tattoo marks upon the lips and chin.   With the grace
of carriage for which Arab women are renowned,
they follow the old man, keeping their eyes fixed on
the ground.

.   .   .   .

To the east, the country tumbles away in a maze of
hills and wadies for a distance of about six miles to a
ridge of jagged peaks, intersected by precipitous
ravines, hiding from view the more distant hills that
slope down to the Jordan Valley.   The whole outlook
is very desolate, and not a single village is to be seen
beyond the one or two quite close at hand.   The low-
lying ground is overhung with morning mists, and away
in the far distance the mountains of Moab and Gilead

loom up like a solid wall. At their foot, a little to the south, the Dead Sea shines with the reflection of a mirror, whilst in the Jordan valley nothing is distinguishable through the white mist that gives it the appearance of an unfathomable gap in the earth's surface. The faint tinge of vermilion in the eastern sky gradually deepens, the red orb of the sun peeps over the wall of mountain, and gaining courage, ascends into the heavens to give us those necessary elementals of life, light and warmth. The effect is wonderful. The ruddy glow travels across the intervening space from height to height, and the permeating warmth cheerily greets you with the heartiness of a friendly slap on the back. From the low-lying recesses among the hills that are spread out at your feet the mists begin to roll away like liquid mother-of-pearl.

Transferring your gaze to the west, the most striking view is obtained, which embraces the entire city of Jerusalem, and fills you with the deepest emotions. The innumerable gravestones that cluster around the walls and crowd the burial grounds in the valley are now more easily seen, and give a mournful aspect to the panorama, which is accentuated rather than diminished by the crumbling decay that is apparent everywhere. The sun throws his powerful rays across Olivet, and licks the dome-roofed houses which are so tightly packed that they look as though they had huddled together during the night for warmth.

.   .   .   .

Turning again to the east, a marvellous transformation scene has taken place. The atmosphere has entirely cleared. So transparent is it, that the smallest detail on the bare hills is visible, and the Dead Sea looks so near that it seems almost possible to throw a

L

stone into it; yet it is many miles away, and three thousand nine hundred feet below the spot where you stand.   More to the north, in the Jordan valley, a double row of broken limestone hills mark the course of the river, but all that can be seen is the dark scrub growing on its banks, effecting a marked contrast to the white hills by which it is hemmed in.

In the evening the view is no less wonderful, for then the blinding glare from the surrounding white hills is subdued, and the exquisite colouring defies the imitating brush of the artist.   The ever-changing shadows among the hills in the middle distance, the delicate mauves of the far-off mountains cut up by the deeper tones of the gorges that debouch into the Dead Sea, and the remarkable clearness of the visibility hold the spectator in thraldom.

The view from Olivet, with its strange beauty and old associations, lives long in the memory, and in after years you never tire of recalling it, and experience a peculiar longing to gaze upon it once more.

.   .   .   .

The Mount of Olives is not always the pleasant and fascinating view point just depicted, for there may come a period, any time from the middle of December to the beginning of February, when it seems the most miserable and wretched place on earth.   This is, of course, in bad weather, and exposed as it is to the four winds, the shelter of stone walls even is not sufficient protection.   But, if you are under canvas or, worse still, in bivouacs, then you can prepare for a very uncomfortable time indeed.   One occasion stands out particularly clearly in my memory.   We had just been relieved from a spell in the line to the east of the mount, and returning to the summit, camped in bell tents on an open space by the road-side.   The weather was bitterly cold, and a prolongation of the rain and wind, which we had endured for a fortnight, seemed certain. Everybody carefully dug drains around the tents to carry off the expected rain, and, hoping for the best, turned in for the night. The peace reigning over a camp shortly before " lights out " has a peculiar charm. Every tent has its one or more candles struggling against the wind to keep alight—the number depending upon how many people have a friend in the Quartermaster's department—and grotesque shadows are cast against the tent walls by men getting into bed. There is a general settling down, and a spirit of cheerfulness prevails. Then the lights are extinguished one by one, the murmuring voices gradually cease, and, save for the sentries pacing up and down, the camp sleeps. On this particular night the camp slept very soundly, for we had had a tiring day, but after a short while—I believe such occasions are timed to happen when the most wakeful have just departed into the land of dreams—a high wind sprang up, and rain and hail began to pelt down. The tents swayed to and fro, the wind howled, and the rain fell in torrents. Grave misgivings were entertained by the awakened men as to whether the pegs would hold, but an unconquerable power possesses you at such a time and causes you to delay braving the night to attend to them. The man by the door is told that it is his job, but he puts forth a dozen reasons why the man opposite should perform the unpleasant task. Everybody thinks somebody else ought to do it, until it is too late. A terrific gust of wind drags up the brailing pegs, another fills the tent, whilst a third reinforces it, and, by their combined efforts, the whole " caboodle " is lifted up like a parachute and carried some distance away, leaving the unhappy occupants and their belongings to be soaked by the pouring rain. This happened not once but a dozen times during this particular night, and as can be imagined, placed many unfortunate fellows in a most miserable plight. The next morning a stranger might have wondered why each tent was surrounded by great rocks and boulders at the end of the guy ropes, but it would have been injudicious to inquire.

During these spells of bad weather the camels and their native drivers suffered severely. A camel camp had been established a little way up the slope of the Mount of Olives from the Kedron Valley, and during heavy rain the water rushed down the hill in rivulets, cutting channels in the sodden earth, and turning the camp into little better than a swamp. The camels were " barracked " in the mud and water, and when not slipping and sliding up or down the hills bringing us supplies, they used to lie there looking the personification of abject misery. Though they were but beasts, they excited the pity of the most hard-hearted. Many died from the cruel conditions which they were unavoidably forced to bear. The native drivers suffered almost as keenly, for they had but a ruined house with no roof to it to shelter them. They were issued dark blue overcoats, which they usually wore over their heads, and stout leather shoes, but as the majority of them had never worn shoes in their lives before, they generally tied these to the camels' saddles, being content to wade through the mud barefooted.

.   ..   .

During a later respite from the line on the Mount of Olives an opportunity was given us to visit Bethlehem. A guard had been supplied at the Church of the Nativity, and our natural curiosity had been whetted by the interesting experiences related by those men whose good fortune it had been to compose that guard. The very name of Bethlehem stirs within you a feeling of deep reverence for the sacred history of the place, and after a moment's reflection, your eagerness to undertake the journey and see it for yourself knows no bounds. I will ask the reader here to accompany us upon such an expedition.

It is a bright sunny morning, though a faint suspicion of winter can still be traced in the air. You descend one of the many steep paths into the Valley of Kedron, the stench of the camels floating up to you in the breeze from the camp below. Passing through the camel camp you cross the valley, and climb another winding path that brings you on to the Jericho road by the north-east corner of the city wall. Here you follow the road along the northern side of the city which leads into Jaffa Street. On the left the massive stone wall rises up like an immense fortress, and on the right there is a hillock covered with fresh green grass, so uncommon a sight in the environs of Jerusalem that it calls for particular attention. On the top are a number of Moslem tombstones, and I never passed that way without being reminded of the hymn which tells of a " green hill far away, without a city wall," for though antagonistic to the generally accepted theory, it seemed to me to answer exactly to this description of Calvary. As a matter of fact, in the latter half of the last century, certain scholars, including Colonel Conder and General Gordon, propounded the theory that this hill is the true site of Our Lord's death, and that the tomb in the cliff near by is the true Holy Sepulchre. This is given weight by the Talmudic description.

Farther along the road a small group of men are

approaching at a very quick pace. You know they are men, for as they hurry along they seem to be chanting in low, gruff voices. They come nearer, and you find they are Jews, poor Jews, dressed in threadbare coats over their gowns of black and yellow stripes, and trousers that hardly reach the tops of their broken boots. They also wear flat, black felt hats that have a clerical resemblance, and long corkscrew curls hang in front of their ears. Two of them appear to be carrying something white, and the others walk on either side and in the rear, their hands clasped behind their backs. The carriers walk one behind the other, and resting on their shoulders is a stout pole. Suspended from the pole is an object wound round and round with white material like sheeting, but the uneven wrappings do not disguise the shape of a human body tied at either end to the pole. As they pass, their pace seems to quicken, and the form swings from side to side in accord with the gait of the carriers. The members of this mournful procession look neither to right nor left, but hurry along with their eyes downcast, chanting in a dismal monotone. Before you realize what it all means, they are away down the road, and the sound of their gruff voices dies away as they turn the corner in the direction of the burial grounds in the valley to the east of the city.

Just before reaching the Damascus Gate, numbers of little children meet you on their way to school. They all speak English, and take a keen delight in greeting you with a cheery " Good morning," a delight which is heightened by your response in making some commonplace remark to which they have a ready reply.

In Jaffa Street the day's business is in full swing. The keepers of cheap souvenir shops stand at their doors to persuade the loitering stranger to step inside

JERUSALEM RAILWAY STATION.

and buy strings of rosary beads or mother-of-pearl knick-knacks; water carriers bend low beneath the weight of the swollen skins that glisten in the sun, motor cyclists race along the thoroughfare with despatches, and motor lorries rumble down the hill with their loads of supplies. Climbing up the steepest part of the hill is a little donkey with a sack of wheat on his back. On the top of the sack sits a lazy Arab, swinging his long legs outwards and in again with every motion of the animal's body, urging it on with weird grunts and ejaculations. Opposite the Jaffa Gate is a tumbledown native café with little tables and rickety chairs placed outside on the cobble stones, where picturesque Bedouins and peasants sit in the warm sun drinking black coffee and playing dámeh (draughts). But you have no time to linger and watch these strange and interesting sights, despite the well-nigh irresistible temptation to do so, for there are six miles of bad road to be covered before you reach your destination. So you turn the corner and proceed down the hill into the Valley of Hinnom, pass the Citadel on your left, on past the Birket es Sultan (the Lower Pool of Gihon, now quite dry) and up the farther slope by the station of the Jaffa-Jerusalem Railway.[1]

Few journeys can compare with the memories and ancient historical connections of these six miles of rough, rutty road. Abraham must have taken this route on his way to Mount Moriah, and two generations later Jacob travelled south and buried his beloved Rachel by the wayside. David secured his

---

[1] The railway was not then in use, for the narrow gauge line had not been converted to accommodate British rolling stock. The Turks had destroyed nearly all rolling stock they were forced to abandon.

victory over the Jebusites in a neighbouring valley, and the splendid retinue of Solomon, no doubt, passed along the road on his many visits to the gardens of Ethan.[1] Over a thousand years later, Joseph and Mary took this path on their way to Bethlehem, and were followed by the Wise Men, who were guided by the star they saw reflected in a well where they rested.

Bethlehem, or Beit-Lahm, " the house of flesh," cannot be dissociated from the tales with which we are familiar from childhood, of Ruth and Boaz, the anointing of David the son of Jesse to be King over Israel, the birth of Christ, and the slaughter of the innocent babes by Herod, tales that have made the name a household word wherever the Christian Faith is professed. As you walk along this ancient road these events engross the whole of your thoughts, banishing, for the time being, the uninteresting scenery around. The scenery does not long remain uninteresting, however, for presently the country-side becomes very picturesque, and the hills and valleys show signs of extensive cultivation, point-ing to a state of prosperity not often encountered in Palestine.

The road winds in and out among the hills, and eventually the City of David is seen straight ahead, crowning the summit of a hill. At a point passed a quarter of an hour before the ascent to the town is commenced, a whitewashed building, surmounted by a dome, stands on the right of the road. Ostensibly, it is just such another building as may be found anywhere in the country, and in the ordinary way would be passed by unnoticed. But it covers

[1] The ancient Jewish law prohibiting the planting of trees within the city is a probable reason for the wise king having his garden elsewhere.

one of the most authentic and ancient sites in the Holy Land, and is acknowledged by Jews, Moslems and Christians.   It is Rachel's Tomb.

A few yards more, and the road forks.   Climbing the winding, uphill branch to the left you enter the main street.   At first the houses are of comparatively modern architecture, but as you progress the street becomes very narrow, and the grey stone buildings on either side assume an appearance of venerable old age.   Again taking a sharp turn, this time to the right, the street ascends a short hill, and the houses, like those of Jerusalem, meet overhead, forming a tunnel through which the street passes.

Canon Tristram in describing Bethlehem says: " The town, no longer walled, is still confined within its ancient limits, and the long narrow street, with various alleys on either side of it, presents us with one of the few remaining specimens of an old Jewish city, for, excepting the disappearance of the walls, it is probably unchanged in architecture and arrangement from what it was in the days of David."

Bethlehem is the most Christian town in Palestine. The Moslem quarter was destroyed by Ibrahim Pasha after a rebellion in 1834.   The women of Bethlehem were by far the best-looking we had seen since leaving Egypt.   Their dress, unlike that of their Moslem sisters, is very picturesque, the outstanding feature being the peculiar high-crowned brimless hats worn by the married women.   They rather resemble flower-pots, and generally are liberally adorned with rows of silver coins.   From this head-dress—for such it is, rather than a hat—a long white veil is suspended, which usually rests in graceful folds on the shoulders, and then falls down the back.

Passing along this quaint old street and through

the tunnel, the object of your visit appears—the Church of the Nativity. This grand old pile of masonry, a most bewildering collection of convents and chapels, is the oldest Christian Church in the world. The original building, constructed under the direction of Helena, the mother of Constantine, in the beginning of the third century A.D., has survived the turbulent times through which the country has passed, and, still unchanged in its main features, stands to-day to enshrine the most hallowed spot on earth. The nave, the original Basilica, is the common property of all Christians, though the adjacent convents and chapels belong to the different sects by whom they were erected.

Outside the entrance—a low archway, barely five feet high—tucked away in a corner, stands an Italian sentry (the guard at the time being supplied by the Italian contingent at Jerusalem) who examines visitors' authorities to enter the Church, a pass signed by the Military Governor-General of Bethlehem or Jerusalem. You have to stoop very low in passing through the doorway to avoid bumping your head, and having successfully escaped an accident, you find yourself in an outer court or covered porch. Passing straight through, you enter the nave, a long, lofty hall with two rows of monolithic columns of red and white marble down either side, forming four side aisles. This is the oldest part of the church, and, presumably because it belongs to no particular sect whose responsibility would be to look after it, the place wears a very dilapidated and almost depressing appearance. Beneath the shabbiness, however, the mosaic decorations on the walls dating from A.D. 1169, and the crests of the Crusaders painted on the shafts, are still discernible. The roof is composed of stout beams of British oak presented by King Edward IV of England.

At this point you are met by a Franciscan monk, a cheery old fellow, the essence of benignity in his chocolate coloured robes, who conducts you down the length of the nave and into a small side chapel. On the floor is a thick carpet, but half of it is doubled over diagonally from corner to corner leaving half the floor bare. The ownership of this chapel is equally divided between the Greeks and the Armenians, and much jealousy exists between the two. The Greeks own the carpet, but, of course, only half the floor area, and when the Armenian Monks sweep their half in the mornings, if the smallest part of the carpet overlaps their territory, as it were, the greatest excitement ensues, the Armenians protesting vehemently until the offending carpet is confined strictly within the prescribed limits.

The Chapel, or Grotto, of the Nativity, is an underground cave over and around which the Church is built. Access to it is gained by passing through an opening in the rock wall and descending a flight of stone stairs. The staircase is very dim, and following your sacerdotal guide, who holds a lighted taper above his head, you cautiously descend the uneven steps which have been worn smooth by the feet of pilgrims for many centuries. The walls of the staircase are hung with tapestries, but by pulling these aside the rough rock is disclosed to view. At the foot of the stairs is a Christian sentry who, bareheaded, stands in the honoured rôle of guardian over this sacrosanct spot, an office which has hitherto been performed by Moslem soldiers. The walls of the cave also are hung with heavy tapestries and ornaments, and suspended by chains from the ceiling are numerous metal lamps of varying shapes and designs, which have been presented at different periods by monarchs and princes of Europe.

On the left is a grotto of marble in which sixteen lamps are hung in a semi-circle. These are filled with oil, and by an ingenious contrivance a wick is supported on the surface of the oil and kept burning night and day.

In the middle of the floor of the grotto a silver star, presented by the French Government, is inlaid, having fourteen points and a sunken centre. This star marks the birthplace of Christ, and pilgrims, in their great faith, fall upon their knees before it and kiss the centre.

The feelings experienced as you contemplate this hallowed spot may be conceived, but they cannot be described. Voices are lowered to a whisper for fear of disturbing the serene silence, and it seems as though this place, above every other on earth, if your religion means anything to you, is all-powerful in influencing the mind to a sensibility of the presence of the Spirit of God.

At the side of the grotto, and fastened to the wall by small brass-headed nails, is an apparatus for lowering the lamps from the ceiling of the cave. One of these nails is missing, and a peculiar story is attached to it. The Greeks, having no part or share in the grotto (for they perform their devotions up a side passage), make it their ambition to supply the missing nail, and by such a contribution entitle themselves to an equal claim to worship there with other sects. The sentry is charged with the duty of on no account to allow this to take place, and the last time an attempt was made the Turkish sentry had perforce to use his bayonet to maintain order. The reason for such unseemly jealousy is rather obscure, but this is all the information to be obtained from the Franciscan monk who shows us round.

In an adjoining cave is another grotto, said by the Latins to be where the manger was discovered. All that can be seen is a marble trough, and some would have you believe that this covers the actual wooden manger in which the infant Christ was laid. But this is not so, for it is lodged in the Church of St. Maria Maggiore at Rome. The back of this grotto is hung with an oil-painting depicting the Wise Men offering their presents to the new-born King. This is only a copy of the original picture which was valued at £30,000 and was stolen some years ago.

Close by, connected by a passage, is the Latin Chapel of St. Joseph, said to be the spot to which Joseph retired, and received the command to fly to Egypt. It contains some very old oil-paintings, but the light is so poor that they cannot be seen to advantage. Passages lead to various caverns, the tombs of friends of St. Jerome, and one, the Tomb of the Innocents, is where some thousands of little victims of Herod's great crime are supposed to be buried. Another passage leads to the Chapel of St. Jerome where that "illustrious champion of the Church" lived for thirty-four years, when he fasted and toiled, revising and translating the Scriptures. In one corner of the cave, high up under the ceiling, is a small grating through which percolate beams of light from the outer world, and blending with the dim glow from the candles on the altar, create a rather depressing tone that pervades the whole chamber.

Whatever the doubts overshadowing the sacred sites of Palestine, it is very possible that the Grotto of the Nativity marks the *exact* spot where Christ *was* born, for the tradition has been handed down since the time of Justin Martyr, one hundred and fifty years after the event. Caves adjacent to inns and used as stables were quite common in those days, in fact, examples may be seen in Palestine and the country east of the Jordan to this day. It is quite easy to conceive that Joseph and Mary arrived at the inn and found it full when we recall that at the time a register of the taxable population was in course of compilation by one, Cyrenius, under the orders of Augustus, the Roman Emperor whom Herod had displeased, and it was required that the people should be enrolled in their paternal towns. Many families had settled elsewhere, so that a general migration took place in order to comply with the registration decree. Among those so situated was Joseph, living at Nazareth, and being of the lineage of David, he journeyed with his wife Mary to Bethlehem.

It is pleasant to believe in the authenticity of traditional sites, and if any error has been made in identifying this one, it cannot be of greater extent than a few yards. Unlike the site of Calvary, which was lost in the chaos following the destruction of Jerusalem by Titus, the place of the Saviour's birth has been preserved and reverenced since the earliest days of Christianity.

An opportunity to visit Bethlehem comes to few of us, and to those few generally but once. As you retrace your steps to Jerusalem the distance covered passes unnoticed, for your mind is concentrated upon the wondrous things you have seen, which open up a hitherto unexplored and neglected region of thought, and make you conscious of having accomplished that which stands as the lifelong ambition of millions of Christians in all parts of the world.

No pilgrimage is complete until a journey has been made down to the banks of Jordan, but the time had not yet come for the extension of our activities to that region, so the completion of our " pilgrimage," and the attendant circumstances, must be reserved for a later chapter.

CHAPTER XVIII

FURTHER OPERATIONS. THE CAPTURE OF JERICHO.
PREPARATIONS FOR CROSSING THE JORDAN (*February
2nd, March 21st,* 1918)

IT soon became manifest that before a further advance
could be made it was imperative that our right flank
should be rendered more secure. The existing bend
in the line to the east of Jerusalem precluded such
further operations, and in order to remove that
disability it would be necessary to drive the enemy
across the Jordan, entailing first his dislodgment from
the ridge of hills that interrupt the general falling
away of the country to the Jordan Valley, and,
secondly, the capture of Jericho. With success the
advantages offered by the resultant situation would be
threefold : any operations by the Turks in the wild
tract of country west of the Dead Sea would be
impossible, we would have control of that sheet of
water, and with access to the crossings of the river the
primary difficulties of our intercepting the communica-
tions of the Turkish Force opposed to the Hedjaz
Arabs, east of the Jordan, would be surmounted.

The task of accomplishing these objects fell to
our Division, as we held the line on the right, and for
the purpose the Australian and New Zealand Mounted
Division (less one Brigade and Artillery) would
co-operate.

With the improved weather conditions in the latter

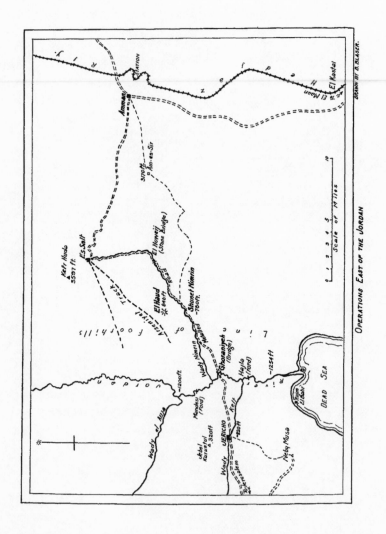

OPERATIONS EAST OF THE JORDAN

half of February, preparations were made to carry out the project. The first thing to be done, therefore, was to capture the ridge of broken hills before referred to, which constituted a very strong defensive position, and much careful observation was necessary to determine which of the summits were occupied and what works or fortifications existed, if any. The extreme left of the enemy's front rested upon a conspicuous hill called El Muntar (Watchtower), the highest point of the ridge, the western slopes of which are split by several long, sweeping spurs. Our Battalion was to work on the right of the British front, capture El Muntar, then change direction left, and work along the ridge to a peculiar cup-shaped hill named Jebel Joffet Sherif, and gradually close in on the centre Brigade before working through the hills eastwards on to the plain below.

We were at this time billeted in the large house of the late Sir John Grey-Hill, on the Mount of Olives, and an observation post was established at the top of the tower of the German Hospice, the Headquarters of the 20th Army Corps. Much enemy movement was observed to the north of El Muntar, particularly centred around Talat ed Dumm, the ruins of a Crusaders' castle, which overlooks the road to Jericho as it worms its way among the hills like a long white snake. Near this spot stood the " Good Samaritan Inn " (Khan Hadrur), a hostel famous amongst travellers to the Jordan Valley for being the only house of call, or of any other kind, between Jerusalem and Jericho, and approximately half-way between the two. The neighbourhood is very desolate, and in pre-war days had the reputation of being infested with bandits, a circumstance necessitating parties of pilgrims being escorted by soldiery.

M

The Turkish Government supplied this protection, actuated, no doubt, by the dual motive of gain and conciliating the Christian powers. Pilgrim caravans used to stop at the " Good Samaritan Inn," where no doubt a body of escorting troops was stationed.

Parties of Turks were frequently seen going to and from the inn, thereby communicating to us the fact that they had made the place their Headquarters. A battery of heavy guns was informed, and one fine morning, after honouring it with persistent attention, the famous inn was reduced to a pile of debris. By their injudicious coming and going the Turks are responsible for the fact that future travellers will now no longer be able to obtain refreshment—even at extortionate prices—from the old inn on their weary journey down to Jordan.

The initial step in the operations was to capture El Muntar on the right and Ras el Tawil, a hill of considerable formidability, opposed by the left Brigade. Our objective was somewhat wrapped in mystery. Very little movement had been observed on the hill or in the immediate neighbourhood, and in the absence of information from other sources, it was impossible to tell in what strength the enemy held it. A mounted patrol had gone out some days previously, but was unable to gather much information beyond a general idea of the approaches, and by working round in a south-easterly direction to the Monastery of Mar Saba, in the lower reaches of the Kedron, had ascertained that the eastern slopes were very steep and rugged. The whole scheme of attack had been worked out from observation, field sketches, and a map which I prepared specially for the occasion, based upon a German map I managed to acquire in Jerusalem. It was just as possible that the hill was held by outposts only, as it was that an ambuscade awaited us in the fastnesses concealed over the crest. Our feelings were in consequence very mixed as to what kind of a task lay before us.

Accordingly, on February 18th, the whole Division moved forward among the maze of wadies intersecting the intervening country, the various Battalions making for their respective points of deployment, entailing a long march over very rough ground.

It was necessary in approaching El Muntar to make a wide detour to the south, following the Wady en Nar for some distance before a tributary was reached affording a passage in the desired direction. A point was reached by the afternoon beyond which it was impossible to move until night fell and a halt of some hours enabled us to obtain food and rest.

At dusk we continued to the point of deployment, and at the popular hour of dawn sallied forth to the attack. An uncanny silence prevailed, counselling us to proceed with caution, so scouts were sent forward to reconnoitre. In one case two of them were carefully approaching a cairn of stones, when suddenly four or five shots were fired from it. The men immediately dropped to the ground for cover, and like good scouts lay perfectly still, but not before one of them was struck by three of the bullets. He had a miraculous escape, for all shots hit some part of his equipment, while he remained unhurt. It seemed he bears a charmed life, as will further be instanced later, when he so brilliantly distinguishes himself on the other side of the Jordan. Pursuing their investigations, the scouts reached the cairn, and found signs of a post, but no enemy. Not another shot was fired. The absence of resistance rendered the position of things the more obscure, but as the leading waves reached the summit it was found that there was no enemy there to resist—a highly satisfactory state of affairs. Objective number one was therefore gained without loss, or, to quote the expression used at the time, was " a walkover." This commenced the rolling up of the enemy's flank, and enabled the cavalry to concentrate behind El Muntar, preparatory to penetrating from the hills on to the plain.

The nature of the country was the most difficult yet encountered during the campaign. The ground was cut up by innumerable wadies and wild precipitous ravines, forming rugged pinnacles and cup-shaped pits impossible to negotiate. So intricate was the geological formation that at one place a field battery had to be helped along by infantry man-handling the guns. The battery took thirty-six hours to cover a distance of eight miles as the crow flies. Not a single tree or bush relieved the entire nakedness, and the whole outlook was desolate in the extreme. Progress was necessarily slow, single-file being the only formation by which we could get along at all, but in due course we reached Jebel Joffet Sherif without coming into contact with the enemy.

During the night the Turks sent out a fighting patrol, which engaged in a sharp skirmish with the centre Brigade, but were soon driven off. They still adhered to the vile practice of stripping our dead and wounded who chanced to fall into their hands—a practice which they adopted extensively during the bad weather before Christmas, when the 18th London Battalion came to grief on Khurbet Adasse, a hill north of Shafat. I saw several bodies of our men lying in the open which had been similarly treated on this occasion. There had as yet been no time to bury them, but some considerate passer-by had reverently covered them over with anything that lay at hand.

On the morning of February 20th the left Battalion of our Brigade attacked Jebel Ektief, which lies between Jebel Joffet Sherif and Talat ed Dumm. With only one way of approach they were confronted with a task the difficulties of which were greatly increased by the stubborn resistance put up by the Turks. By their determined assault the position was stormed and carried by midday. Earlier in the morning, the centre Brigade, in spite of considerable opposition, captured Talat ed Dumm on the Jericho road, whilst on the left, the stronghold of Ras el Tawil likewise fell before the tenacious onslaughts of the left Brigade. To the north, the 53rd Division simultaneously extended its right to Rummon, in order to keep in touch. The fighting at these three points was severe.

The enemy were now being pushed eastwards on to the Jericho Plain, and our cavalry advancing from the south threatened their flank, leaving them the one alternative of retiring on the Jordan. This was not done until they had made themselves very objection-able to the mounted men by hampering their further progress with guns stationed at Neby Musa. A way out of the hills was eventually discovered, whereupon the Turks made off.

Neby Musa is a large shrine, built by the Moslems over the spot where they hold Moses was buried. The building viewed from the hills resembles a large square monastery, its outstanding feature being many white domes. As the day lengthened, the gathering clouds overhead foretold rain, but as Neby Musa was

to be our destination, good prospects were entertained
of spending the night under cover. Fair progress
was made, with no signs of the enemy, and towards
evening the white domes came in sight far below on a
plateau just above the plain. Some distance to the
south, making in the same direction, was a large body
of New Zealand Mounted Rifles, no doubt also holding out prospects of sheltering in the building. It
was simply a question as to who would reach the goal
first. Our Colonel, readily taking in the situation,
determined that we should not be outdone, and
ordered the pace to be so increased that the Battalion
was practically running a race with the horsemen for
the night's billet. Distance and other considerations
were in our favour, so we won, the New Zealanders
having to bivouac in the open. The rain was only
slight, however, so no discomforts were experienced.
The building was quite deserted, but that the Turks
had been in recent occupancy was evidenced by the
filth and rubbish which they habitually left behind
them.

On the day following we consolidated a line about
a mile north of Neby Musa. The term "consolidate"
is very comprehensive, and used in this connection
has a meaning that no dictionary explains. First and
foremost, the Commanding Officer surveys the general
position, picks out the points of strategical value, and
decides to establish a post at each. Five minutes
afterwards a group of temporary navvies is seen
engaged on excavations with implements invented for
the purpose. In time these excavations develop into
trenches, and in some of them machine guns are
placed. Then along comes the Battalion map-maker,
who takes innumerable forward-bearings, cross-
bearings and back-bearings, and ranges in all

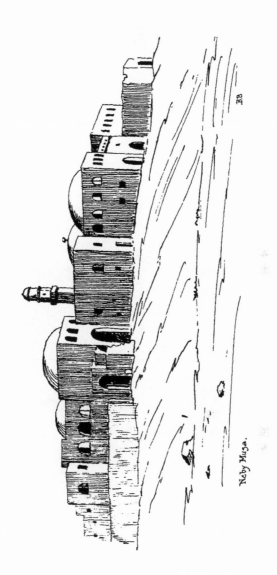

Neby Musa.

directions with instruments suspended in leather
cases from his neck, and makes mysterious signs on
a roll of paper ruled in squares, impressing the men
working near with his learning. He is a man it
is well to know, and whose friendship is worth
cultivating, for he is reckoned, however erroneously,
a fountain of knowledge. He is plied with such
questions as: " Where are we? " " Where are *they?* "
" What's that place over there? " and " How long are
we going to stay here? " If he is wise his replies are
non-committal, but to assure his interrogators that the
war is not yet over, he unrolls a few yards of map
displaying an apparently enormous stretch of territory
yet to be covered. More or less satisfied, the diggers
continue to dig to the refrain of:

> " Another little ridge, another little ridge,
> Another little ridge won't do us any harm,"
> etc., etc.,

while others facetiously compare us with " globe-
trotters " and " Cook's tourists." Those who are not
digging erect bivouacs on selected pitches, and proceed
to make themselves comfortable. They are experts
at this, for they do it *so* often; sometimes twice a day.
It is an unfailing rule when campaigning that as soon
as you have settled down, and are comparatively
comfortable, you will get orders to move. But you
get used to this, and come to consider it " all in a
day's march."

At Neby Musa we were in the Jordan Valley, some
miles south of Jericho, and the new aspect presented
was extremely dreary. Jericho itself was obscured
from view by a projecting cliff, but to the north-east,
the east, and right round to the south, the plain
stretched like a map, gradually sloping down to the
Jordan. Not a single object of interest was to be seen

until one became accustomed to the monotony, when with the aid of field-glasses the Monastery of Kasr Hajlah could be discerned in the bare, dusty expanse. Far away to the east, through the midday haze, rose the Mountains of Gilead like a huge long shadow, and in the south the Dead Sea glistened in the sun. The plain was absolutely flat except for the limestone hills that appeared like a white streak running down the centre marking the course of the Jordan. A cavalry patrol was nearing Hajlah, but was soon lost to view in the haze, which rendered the visibility very poor.

The Turks had retired across the Jordan by means of the El Ghoraniyeh bridge, which they were covering from the left bank with guns. To the north the plain was clear of the enemy as far as the Wady el Aujah, which leaves the hills and follows a south-easterly course across the plain to the Jordan, about eight miles north of where that river enters the Dead Sea. Here again the Turks had taken up positions on the left bank.

The first phase of the operations being now completed, we were ordered to withdraw from the valley, leaving one brigade of mounted men to carry out patrol duties.

We marched back to Jerusalem by way of the carriage road from Neby Musa, which toils up the hills by a very winding route and joins the Jericho road. On the latter road we overtook crowds of refugees from Jericho, who were making their way to Jerusalem. They had all the belongings they could take with them, including goats and sheep, and a few angular cows. Near Talat ed Dumm we camped for the night, and continued the following morning. The road was in a shocking state of repair, and the Turks had blown up all the culverts in their retreat, which caused the transport much trouble. The road ascends the Mount of Olives by a series of zig-zag stretches with dangerous hair-pin bends, and passes through El Aziriyeh, built on the site of ancient Bethany. I was curious to see what the modern village is like. As with most Arab villages it is disappointing, and comprises but a few straggling stone dwellings built on the hill on either side of the road, and is extremely dirty.

We returned from the operations the same strength as when we set out, not having lost a single man—a circumstance which had never occurred before, nor has since—and as we marched past the German Hospice on the way to our old camping-ground on Olivet, General Sir Phillip Chetwode, our Corps Commander, stood at the gateway and took the salute.

The next day we marched along the Nablus road, turned off to the right by Er Ram, and reached Ras el Tawil, where we took over the line. Just at this period we experienced another spell of bad weather. Rain poured down in torrents, while the wind was bitingly cold. Rough roads had been made by the troops who captured the ground, but these were inches deep in mud. Camels were in a pitiful plight, slipping down at every turn, where they remained in the mud until their loads could be taken off. Some went hurtling over precipices down to their death, while others were lying about with broken legs until they could be shot, so that we were forced to rely almost entirely upon that stupid, contrary, aggravating though sure-footed beast, the mule. Fortunately, this weather lasted only for a few days, and was followed by beautiful clear skies and bright warm sunshine, which soon removed all traces of the recent inclemency and helped us to forget our late troubles. Spring had really come at last, and in my wanderings whilst endeavouring to push the landscape into something like order on our maps, I happened upon many a peaceful, secluded ravine where everything seemed to be again bursting into life, and many a valley scarlet with carpets of anemones.

After we had been at Ras el Tawil for about a week orders were received that we were no longer to pay heed to our present front, but were to concentrate our whole attention on the Jordan Valley. This was immediately followed by a company being dispatched to Mount Quarantania, or Kuruntul, a hill with precipitous sides rising abruptly from the plain and overlooking Jericho. This predicted the commencement of phase two of the general scheme of operations previously outlined.

Two other scouts and myself were ordered to proceed down on to the plain, and thence to a hill two miles north of Jericho called Osh el Ghurab. We were to keep a strict watch on the Jordan, and particularly upon the Mandesi Ford, and were to make sketches showing the wadies affording cover in approaching that ford. Our way took us past the old site of Jericho, the ancient City of Palms. A few crumbling mounds with signs of recent excavations, two large reservoirs now called Ain es Sultan, fed by an aqueduct from the Wady Nueiameh, a tumble-down mill and a clump of poplars completes all that now represents the one-time magnificent city. The sun was extremely warm, and we could not resist the temptation to halt here and enjoy a most delightful bathe in one of the reservoirs.

In due course we reached our destination and formally took possession. Osh el Ghurab is a hill culminating in a sharp point about three hundred feet above the plain, and is isolated from the higher ground to the west. It is said that on this hill Elijah was fed by the ravens whilst in hiding from Ahab. With as little ostentation as possible we got out our materials and instruments, rigged up a telescope, and set to work. The old official maps we had were of little use owing to their inaccuracy, and rather suggested, with all due deference to the men who made them, that the landscape had indulged in a game of "general post" since it was last surveyed. However, we arrived at an amicable understanding with the various features and were soon absorbed in our work.

From the foot of the hill stretches the bare plain cut up by dry wady beds that pursue their continually changing courses down to the white hills enclosing the Jordan. The Nueiameh, the only one hereabouts containing water, is marked by an occasional bush or tree straining to look over the side as though to see what is happening on the plain.

Away to the right near Jericho a flock of black goats wandered aimlessly about, now closing in together and then spreading again, the shrill shepherd-cries of the Bedouin children who tended them travelling through the still air. Many white streaks denoted paths that cross and recross each other in the foreground, one, the broadest and straightest of all, being the roadway leading down to the Ghoraniyeh bridge. Right out in front, perhaps three miles away, a cloud of dust rose where a cavalry patrol was coming in; that was all. For the rest the plain was dead, and ordinary interest in it ceased. You might, perhaps, gaze upon it a little longer if you recalled that this is the ground over which the children of Israel passed on their entry into the Promised Land, and that this dreary plain saw the first of the battles fought under Joshua against the Canaanites. These old associations are not without their appeal to the imagination, but even they will not hold you long, for the place is a wilderness. The patrol came nearer, and the telescope was aligned in order to watch its progress. The Turks across the river had also seen it, for the treacherous cloud of dust gave it away. A shell came whining through the air, and burst a hundred yards to the right. Another landed the same distance in front, and the horsemen separated, each taking a different line, but all taking care to avoid a dead tree trunk upon which a range could be taken. Still another shell was fired. The range was this time much over-estimated, and the shell burst with a sigh at the foot of our hill. After this the gunners gave it up, thus enabling the cavalry to return in peace to their Headquarters near Jericho.

Night was now fast approaching and all was still. As soon as darkness fell, the red glow of fires could be seen in the Turk's territory, the directions of which we carefully marked that bearings might be taken in the morning. We made ourselves as comfortable as possible on a ledge a little way down the hill, and prepared to go through the night with our lonely vigil.

The silence was intense, and notwithstanding that as far as we were then aware the nearest Turks were three miles away, the magic hand of night so touched our imagination and magnified every sound, that we moved about with the utmost caution, lowered our voices to whispers, and breathed almost by stealth. If the three of us had shouted in chorus, the chances were that not a soul could have heard us, though we learned the next morning that it was just as well we remained quiet. If my memory serves me well it was the night of the 6th—7th of March, and just about

(*Upper*) "D" COMPANY OF THE "LONDON SCOTTISH" LEAVING ES SALT, MARCH 27TH, 1918.

(*Lower*) JEBEL KURUNTUL (MOUNT OF TEMPTATION) AND JORDAN VALLEY, LOOKING NORTH.

Photographs by Capt. R. M. Robertson, M.C.

midnight a dull roar came across the valley from the direction of Ghoraniyeh, followed by the reflection of what must have been a very large fire. The Turks had blown up the wooden bridge, the only one for some miles farther north. This was not unexpected, and a note was duly made for the purpose of our report.

During the following morning a party of horsemen appeared from the north on the plain below. Coming from that direction we at first looked upon them with suspicion, but a closer scrutiny showed them to be New Zealanders. In this we had the advantage, for although they could see us on the hill, we judged from their gestures and hesitation that they were by no means sure of our identity. We semaphored to them this intelligence, whereupon they rode round to the side of the hill and dismounted in a re-entrant. Leaving one man in charge of the horses the remainder of the party, composed of an officer, a sergeant and three troopers, joined us. They expressed their astonishment at finding us there, and looked almost incredulous on learning that we had been there all night. Upon first noticing us they had entertained serious thoughts of shooting us, but our message was sent just in time. They told us that we were absolutely isolated, and that parties of Turks mounted on mules and donkeys were in the habit of working down the plain, keeping close in to the foothills to get what information they could. In broad daylight this did not trouble us very much, though if we had been told the night before it might have caused us some concern. The officer posted two troopers on neighbouring points of vantage to watch the wadies in our rear, but after an hour they returned and reported that all was quiet. We chatted for a while and drank cold tea left from breakfast, after which our visitors departed, undertaking to inform their relief party of our whereabouts.

We carried on throughout the day, and gained useful information relating to enemy movements on the other side of the river. Several suspected posts were located, and a way down to the Mandesi Ford from the opposite side of the river was discovered. We were led to the discovery by a black figure— appearing no larger than a pin's head through the telescope—moving on the white hills, and after having traversed what was apparently a pathway, it descended by a projecting spur to the dark scrub growing on the river bank, and was there lost to sight. The points of appearance and disappearance were duly noted on a diagram, and attention was concentrated thereon. Presently two more figures were seen following the same route, also descending to the river. The spot was exactly opposite the Mandesi Ford, so having once effected a crossing, a way up on to the plain was assured. Further observation confirmed the existence of a pathway, and soon more figures were seen moving about where the others had first appeared. A faint coil of smoke also was seen issuing from the spot, suggesting a post or camp, while the men going down the pathway were no doubt on their way to the river for water.

At dusk a messenger arrived with orders for us to withdraw, so gathering our impedimenta we left our lonely pinnacle and returned to the Battalion, which had encamped on the plain near where the Jerusalem road emerges from the hills. The night was very sultry, though the clear sky was studded with bright stars. At Ain es Sultan we again enjoyed a refreshing bathe in the reservoir. We reached the camp to find that the Battalion, with the exception of the sick and a guard, were away carrying out a series of patrols in the neighbourhood of the Mandesi Ford. Dawn would see their return, so we pitched bivouacs, prepared our report, and put the final touches to the sketches.

The next day the Battalion moved up on to the summit of Kuruntul (the Mount of Temptation). An observation post was established, and a rigid look-out kept on the Jordan and the country eastward. The Colonel summoned me and gave me instructions to prepare a large-scale map of the Jordan from aerial photographs. This was to extend from Kasr el Yehud a point five miles north of where the river enters the Dead Sea, to the junction of the Wady el Aujah and Jordan, a stretch of some six miles. The eastern plain as far as the foothills was also to be included, and the western approaches to the various fords and El Ghoraniyeh. Happily the photographs were " jig-sawed " together, set true north, and marked with the representative fraction calculated upon the altitude at which they were taken. The preparation of a map of these dimensions without access to the ground was no mean task, but with the aid of the photographs and continual observation from the post I made good headway.

The view from the top of Kuruntul is second only to that from the Mount of Olives. Rising some nine hundred to a thousand feet sheer, the hill dominates the village of Eriha (the modern Jericho), and completely commands the Jordan Valley to a very considerable distance north and south. At no point can the actual river be seen, for it is hidden by the broken limestone hills that seem as if they are a natural formation to prevent the rushing waters from flooding the plain.   As you stand on the summit and face due east, Jericho lies at your feet far below, an oasis in the desert.   The village is composed of straggling mud huts and shanties, and some half-dozen stone buildings, which threaten at any time to follow the example of the walls of the ancient city. One house proudly exhibits the inscription in large lettering, " Jordan Hotel," though its dirty condition and objectionable surroundings do not recommend it. The inhabitants of Jericho are a very low type of Bedouin-Arab, very dark of skin and questionable of morals.   They are the only people able to live in this unhealthy valley all the year round, and are said to be descended from a Canaanitish tribe.

A little way down the precipice, built in the cliff face, is the Greek Monastery of Quarantania (Forty Days), with a chapel erected over the spot where Christ is supposed to have endured the Temptation. One afternoon I obtained leave to go down to Ain es Sultan to bathe, so took the opportunity of paying a visit with my sketch-book to the monastery.   From our camp a wady full of boulders and sharp stones created a deep cleft in the hill, ending abruptly on the cliff face with a drop of about eight hundred feet to the plain.   Round the left-hand bluff an aqueduct had been constructed in the rock, cemented here and there in weak places to carry rain-water to the monastery.   By cautiously picking your way along this aqueduct—a mere groove in the side of the precipice—and clinging tightly to the projections overhead at the particularly dangerous spots, a short cut is possible, saving a couple of miles or so.   It is necessary to pass along a passage-like street cut in the rock behind the monastery, and down a flight of steep steps, from whence a zig-zag path takes you to the plain below. Doors open from the street into self-contained apartments, more like alms-houses, occupied by the monks, while at the far end is an open door leading to a room in which visitors are received.

In the centre of the room was a square deal table covered with a cloth whose visit to the laundry was long overdue. A water-bottle occupied the centre, the contents of which I found delightfully cool and refreshing. The walls were adorned with gaudy pictures of saints, and a portrait of King Edward VII when Prince of Wales. Through the window it seemed as though there was nothing but space, but on approaching closer the plain appeared, a tremendous distance below. A door led on to a wooden balcony, and the uncomfortable thought flashed through my mind that if the floor suddenly gave way there would be nothing to break my fall for several hundred feet. A little to the right was the southern bluff of Kuruntul. The solitude was immense, but as I gazed out across the plain several great griffin vultures swept majestically through the gorge, and alighted upon a ledge of rock, where they quarrelled over the prey just captured.

The one-roomed apartments each have a balcony overhanging the precipice. Seated on the balcony next to that on which I stood was an old monk studying the landscape through a pair of antiquated field-glasses. I looked out in the direction engaging his attention, and saw an Australian armoured car which had ventured closer to the Jordan than had pleased the Turks, who manifested their disapproval by shelling it. At every explosion the old monk exhibited the greatest concern, and suddenly, noticing my presence, appealed to me as to whether they were " Toor-r-k." I conveyed to the old gentleman that

N

the shells *were* "Toor-r-k," and as they were two miles away I felt justified in evincing contempt for the same by appropriate gestures.   At this he appeared satisfied, and addressed me in Greek, but without effect.   He then tried Russian, with no more success. Not speaking English, he attempted to penetrate my apparently dull understanding with French, which he might as well have done in the first place.   I was then able to gather something of his meaning, and to my astonishment he was asking most pointed questions regarding our intentions to cross the Jordan.   He was no doubt innocent enough of any ulterior motive, but not knowing then who he was, I adopted the safest course in the circumstances of professing ignorance. It is always well to be on your guard against such interrogation, for strangers whose *bona fides* it would seem absurd to doubt have often turned out to be enemy agents.   Perceiving that I could not, or would not, give him much information he desisted in his inquiries.

The old monk made a picturesque figure, and contemplating him sitting there reminded me of my sketch-book.   Upon intimating that I wished to sketch him he readily acquiesced.   After a little difficulty I got him to assume the required pose; but he proved a bad sitter.   He persisted in following, through his field-glasses, the movements of the armoured car which was still careering over the plain, and did not appreciate that it was desirable he should keep still.   Ten minutes sufficed, however, to commit an impression to paper, and reaching across the space between the two balconies, I handed him the book that he might inspect the result.   Upon his expressing his approval I asked him to append his autograph, which he did, writing in modern Greek and adding his

THE CHIEF MONK, KURUNTUL MONASTERY,
MOUNT OF TEMPTATION.

rank, the date, and his age.   I afterwards learned, to my surprise, that he was none other than an Archimandrite.   Highly satisfied with my acquisition I bade him adieu and returned to the visitors' room.

Here I was confronted by a lay brother, in appearance very hairy, dark, and, I thought, dirty. Apart from these personal peculiarities I found him a very pleasant fellow, and he offered to show me over the chapel.   Nothing loath I followed him, returning past all the little alms-houses and into the larger buildings at the other end of the narrow street.   The chapel is not large, but is quite tastefully decorated and cosily furnished.   My attention was particularly attracted by the wooden chairs in which the monks sit during the services.   They are so narrow that they seem incapable of seating an ordinary-sized man; they have tip-up seats, are clamped together in rows, and look much more suitable for children.   Up a flight of stone steps behind the altar is a large stone in shape and size resembling an arm-chair.   This, I was told, was the scene of Christ's Temptation, but the tradition only dates back from the Crusades.   That this may be the actual mountain whereon Christ experienced those tragic moments gains credence, perhaps, by the numerous caves by which the eastern face of Kuruntul is honeycombed.   These caves frequently have an inner chamber or vault serving as a chapel, with frescoes which Canon Tristram ascribes to a period before the canonization of St. Jerome. For generation after generation the caves have been occupied by hermits, who have spent long periods there in solitary meditation.   Even to-day devout men still come from great distances every Lent and there keep their forty days' fast.   Some of the higher caves are no longer accessible, owing to the wearing away of the narrow pathways.

.   .   .   .

In due course the time arrived for launching our expedition across the Jordan. It was to be carried out more in the sense of a gigantic raid, with no intention of maintaining a permanent line. The Hedjaz Arabs had made good progress, having advanced a considerable distance northwards, and had raided Kerak, a town about five miles south of the peculiar peninsular that disturbs the uniformity of outline of the Dead Sea on its eastern shore. If we could so interfere with the lines of communication of their Turkish opponents as to jeopardize the retirement of that force, considerable assistance would be given to our Arab Allies, enabling them to advance farther north into line with our right flank. The Turks were solely reliant upon the railway from Amman for supplies, and the destruction of that railway was the object of the undertaking. To this end a tunnel south of Amman was to be blown up, and as much of the railway line destroyed as possible.

A most unfortunate occurrence took place just at this time, which necessitated a considerable alteration in the plans for crossing the river. One night when our battalion was carrying out patrol work to the Mandesi Ford, a young, inexperienced officer, a Corporal and four men, two of whom were Company scouts, were left hidden in the thick scrub on the river bank to watch and listen during the next day.

Some or one of the party evidently moved from the place of concealment, with the result that the Turks on the opposite bank detected their presence, and immediately opened fire. The officer and some of the men were wounded. One man effected his escape, and returned to report the incident. A later search confirmed our fears that the Turks would cross the river and make the remainder of the party prisoners.

This incident undoubtedly acted as a fore-warning to the enemy of our intentions regarding the ford, so that the project as far as it was concerned had to be abandoned. Two other points were ultimately decided upon as suitable for the crossing, i.e., Ghoraniyeh and Hajlah. Pontoons and other bridging material were taken down by night and concealed in the broken hills close to the scene of operations.

We had been informed that there would be a lot of hard marching before us, and to render us as mobile a body as possible, packs and entrenching tools were left behind with the battalion's stores, whilst great-coats and blankets, tightly rolled in bundles, were carried on camels. Thus relieved, the load we had to carry, even taking into account bivouacking gear, was reduced to a minimum. Just before dusk on March 21st we struck camp, and descending by way of a broad track that winds its way down from the hills, reached the plain near Jericho.

CHAPTER XIX

WE CROSS THE JORDAN. THE RAID ON THE HEDJAZ
RAILWAY. AT ES SALT. THE WITHDRAWAL (*March
22nd, April 2nd,* 1918)

HOWEVER cold the weather may be at Jerusalem,
the climate in the Jordan Valley is always warm and
sultry, and in the summer becomes unbearably hot
and extremely unhealthy. As has been so frequently
pointed out, the great valley is a depression of over
1,200 feet at the southern end, whilst the mean depth
of the Dead Sea adds a further 1,080 feet to this, the
deepest fissure in the earth's crust. From Jericho
to Jordan, a distance of about five miles, the descent is
only 500 feet, whilst during the journey of 15 miles
from Jerusalem to Jericho the traveller descends something like 3,100 feet.

The evening on which we set out upon the
enterprise, although early in the year, was close and
oppressive. Soon after starting it got quite dark,
and the sky became overcast. We followed the Wady
Nueiameh for about three miles, and rested. One
Company proceeded to Ghoraniyeh in support of the
19th, the Battalion detailed to effect a crossing there,
but all attempts to cross the torrent were frustrated by
the current and the enemy's rifle fire. At Hajlah
repeated efforts were made by the 180th Brigade, and
one gallant Sergeant, after several efforts, was mortally
wounded, whilst in the water, by the Turkish fire

from the left bank. Eventually a rope was fastened
to the other side, and the leading Battalion was ferried
over. A further obstacle had then to be faced in the
dense scrub growing down to the water's edge, and
before progress could be made a path had to be cut
through it. The New Zealand engineers succeeded,
in spite of the heavy fire, in constructing a pontoon
bridge, over which a regiment of cavalry crossed at
dawn, and, driving the enemy northwards, secured
the bridge-head at Ghoraniyeh.

Whilst all this was in progress we left the Wady
Nueiameh, and crossed the plain in artillery formation
to the Wady Kelt, where the Brigade was concentrated.
Further attempts to bridge the river at Ghoraniyeh,
on the night of the 22nd proving futile, we had perforce to remain in the Kelt until the morning of
the 23rd, when we marched to Hajlah. As we were
approaching the river a large motor-car passed us,
travelling in the opposite direction. In it sat the
Commander-in-Chief. His presence on the very scene
of operations at such a critical time showed a fine
example to the troops, and evoked general admiration.
In the evening we crossed the Jordan.

In passing over the swaying, trembling pontoons,
with the swollen waters rushing underneath, it seems
hardly credible that this can really be the great
Jordan River. Once realizing that it is no other,
you experience a thrill, and glance from right to left,
in order not to miss any detail, for there is no time to
stop and ponder. One lucky fellow, enjoying a
refreshing bathe in the muddy water, was the object
of many an envious glance; he was an engineer, and
his job was done, whilst ours lay far ahead; and we
passed on. The ground on the other side was very
boggy. The pathway cut through the undergrowth

was paved with logs and branches, but, notwithstanding this it was little better than a quagmire. Having cleared the hills, and gained the eastern plain, we turned north and marched towards Ghoraniyeh. This unavoidable diversion from the original plan had necessitated our marching something like twelve miles, so that we were considerably fatigued when, soon after dusk, we halted in some broken ground, still about three miles from our destination. By the light of the early moon, water was issued. Even at this distance from the Dead Sea the grey earth is encrusted with salt, and in the bright moonlight sparkles as though thickly besprinkled with diamonds. The night was very warm; in fact, oppressive, and we lay down without cover of any kind and slept soundly for almost four hours. Whilst it was yet dark on the 24th, we were again afoot, and reached Ghoraniyeh. Concealed in the Wady Nimrin, we waited for the order to go forward to the attack.

From Ghoraniyeh a carriage road crosses the plain on its way to Es Salt, entering the hills at Shunet Nimrin. Three miles north of Shunet Nimrin rises the high and rugged hill, El Haud, between which two points the Turkish line was established. The main body of cavalry were to work through the hills to Amman, along the track south of the main road, *via* Ain es Sir, a small village inhabited by seven hundred and fifty Circassians, reputed to be hostile, whilst our Brigade and one regiment of cavalry were to advance on Es Salt by way of the Arseniyet Track, north of El Haud. The remaining infantry of the Division, artillery, field ambulances and pack transport, were to proceed to Es Salt by the road, and thence on to Amman, that being the only route by which the latter place could be reached by road.

(*Upper*) PONTOON BRIDGES ACROSS THE JORDAN.
(*Lower*) TRANSPORT EN ROUTE BETWEEN JERUSALEM AND JERICHO.

Es Salt lies approximately on the highest point of the Mountains of Gilead, and is about nineteen miles north-east from Ghoraniyeh by road. Amman is some fifteen miles from Es Salt in an east south-eastern direction. From this it will be seen that our occupation of Es Salt would create an acute salient. As the road through the town constituted our main line of communication, it was imperative that this should be protected, and the task of holding the place was entrusted to our Brigade.

At 9 a.m. the infantry emerged from the Wady Nimrin, and advanced across the plain towards the respective objectives, ours being El Haud. Like the western plain, that on the eastern side is absolutely flat. Although a certain amount of cover was afforded by shrubs and bushes, the enemy could not fail to detect our approach, and soon opened fire with his guns from Shunet Nimrin. After negotiating a field of tall, thickly-growing maize, we deployed and advanced in waves. The positions of the Turks were most formidable, but were not held by sufficient numbers to offer a resistance of any magnitude. Accordingly, the foothills were taken with only a few casualties, and about fifty Turks and Germans captured. Those of the enemy who effected their escape retired into the hills, and gave us no further trouble. On the right more opposition was met, but eventually the guns which had fired on us as we crossed the plain were captured, the gunners shot, and the remainder of the Turkish force retired along the road to Es Salt.

We then commenced a long and tedious climb to the summit of El Haud, where outposts were established for the night.

During the night the weather changed for the

worse, and heavy rain added to the difficulties before us.

Withdrawing from the top of El Haud next morning, we descended the northern slopes, which are steep and difficult, the Brigade concentrating at the mouth of the gorge, through which the Arseniyet Track passes. In spite of the heavy rain our gallant cooks lit fires, and made tea. Rations and water were issued, and we snatched a hasty meal of our staff of life, bully-beef and biscuits. This finished, everything was again packed up, loads once more put on the pack animals, and in single file the whole Brigade set off to Es Salt, prepared for any eventualities.

The Arseniyet Track is a mere bridle-path, following for the first six miles the Wady Meidan in a gradual and continuous ascent. Before the road was constructed this was the route used by caravans and travellers on horseback, but having now fallen into disuse it is in places overgrown with weeds, and difficult to follow. In other places the hills close in on either side confining the track to a narrow defile, great projecting bluffs tower above, continually altering the course, the track itself winding in and out among the rocks and boulders with which it is strewn. Occasionally the hills open out into pleasant green valleys, harbouring a few terebinths or wild almond trees. Here the stately heron is to be found, usually with his mate, and upon our disturbing the quiet of their secluded domain they rose from the ground, gliding gracefully, screeching and crying in protest. After about three hours the wady ends abruptly, and the path mounts the hillside by a steep ascent which occupies half an hour. Across a plateau and round a sharp bend the track again enters a defile. The country here is very wild and rugged, with not a sign of mankind, nor any inducement for him to fix his abode there. Towards midday the rain ceased, but everything was saturated, rendering the going very heavy and laborious. Higher, and still higher, the path ascends through deep ravines, round projecting hills and over rocky spurs, until, after some six hours of tortuous climbing, a large cultivated plateau is reached. The sodden ground squelched under foot, and our boots weighed several pounds heavier with the sticky mud that clung to them. Always on the look-out for new scenes and fresh impressions, I chanced to look back as we mounted on to the plateau. A glance of a few seconds only was sufficient to take in a view which is still fresh in my memory. Far below was the Jordan Valley; a dark rich belt of vegetation ran down the centre, framing the winding river that showed up like silver in the evening light. To the south was the Dead Sea, a great glassy lake, unruffled by wave or ripple, hemmed in on either side by walls of mountain. Columns of smoke emanated from the camps around Jericho, and beyond to the west rose the hills of Judea. The wavy outlines of the ridges showed up clearly, one behind the other, each higher than the one before, and all dominated by the highest, the Mount of Olives. The whole scene was enveloped by the fascinating light that immediately precedes dusk, subdued, but very clear, and in the western sky a streak of vermilion relieved the monotony of the grey clouds. Silhouetted against the sky stood the great tower of the German Hospice, dwarfed in perspective, but there, as always, to dog our footsteps, and magnify the distance we had come.

Night overtook us while we were yet some distance from Es Salt, and progress was necessarily slower.

The sky had cleared after the rain, and a bright moon shone. It became very cold, but this can easily be understood, for we had ascended over four thousand feet since leaving the Jordan. The hourly halts were a mixed blessing for, hot with marching, we would lie down and shiver. Frequently these halts lengthened into twenty minutes' duration or longer, owing to uncertainty as to the route, or a block occasioned by the collapse of a camel. Much difficulty was experienced in getting the creatures over rugged spots, for they were in a foreign element and, in short, proved a hindrance. Signs of cultivation began to appear, vineyards, olives, and fig trees were passed, showing us that we had not far to go. We fell in with some Australian cavalrymen, who told us that the town had been occupied. The force moving along the road had naturally got there first, and the Turks, offering but slight opposition, had evacuated. As we drew nearer rifle shots were heard some distance away, but seemingly in all directions, which puzzled us considerably. Always disturbing to a soldier's peace of mind that ominous sound promotes feelings of alarm if the cause or origin remains unexplained; but we pressed on, being too tired to pay any heed to the otherwise disquieting reports. The ground became rougher and stonier than ever, but eventually, when it seemed that we could really climb no higher, we halted on a stretch of ploughed land. On the heavy sodden earth we pitched our bivouacs, and, after gulping down an issue of raw rum, lay down to spend one of the most wretched nights in our experience. The camels carrying our greatcoats and blankets were some miles back, the ground being too rough for them to proceed farther. By spreading out the contents of our packs and the empty packs themselves, we managed to get some protection from the wet earth. The hillside was over-hung with a white mist that chilled to the bone, and although dog-tired no sleep came to help us to forget our misery. All through the night the intermittent firing continued to arouse the dulled senses into a belief that we were being attacked, but we shivered the night through and gladly welcomed the dawn, cold and raw though it was.

As the mists cleared away, the town of Es Salt appeared down in the hollow. Of its fifteen thousand inhabitants one-third are Christians, the remaining two-thirds being composed of Circassians, and a particularly war-like type of Bedouin—Arabs who detest any organized system of government, preferring to submit to the authority of local Sheikhs. We had previously been warned of their war-like tendencies, that it was the custom for all men to go about armed, and that we were not to interfere with them or attempt to take their fire-arms from them. During the morning their fighting spirit was amply illustrated, and at the same time cleared up the mystery of the firing in the night. Shots rang out continually from the town, and later, a band of young men came up to our camps manifesting their approval of the altered condition of affairs by firing their rifles in the air. It was an infectious complaint, for no sooner did one wild young Bedouin fire, than his friends all followed suit in the exuberance of their good feeling towards us and their high spirits generally. To humour them we cheered and clapped, at which they laughed boisterously and repeated the performance, not being at all particular in which direction they pointed their rifles nor careful of the ultimate destination of the bullets. The rifles were of various makes, from antiquated native pro-ductions to the latest British and German patterns.

The majority were German and Turkish. Some of these "young bloods" wore machine gun belts filled with cartridges wound round their waists, over their shoulders and across their chests, but their faces seemed to wear a sad and woeful expression. It was noticeable that they were not deriving the maximum of pleasure from their rifles; in fact, many were not attempting to fire at all. The reason for their despondency was explained upon their quietly sidling up to us, and by signs and rolling of eyes, expressing their desire to possess some British ammunition. They had British rifles, probably stolen from the Turks, but the thousands of rounds encasing their bodies like suits of armour were German. We were, of course, forbidden to supply their wants in this direction, and at night had to sleep with our rifles and ammunition close at our sides owing to the propensities of these gentry for illicitly acquiring other people's property.

An opportunity to go down to Es Salt came along, of which a companion and I quickly availed ourselves. The place was very filthy. It occupies a site situated at the junction of several wadies, and the houses, crowded together on the hill slopes, appear to be built one on top of the other. In the centre of the town stands a fountain where volumes of pure sparkling water gush forth into stone troughs. This is the water supply for the whole community. Crowds of troops were filling innumerable water-bottles, which they hung on mules, and sombrely clad native women and girls were filling their pitchers for domestic use. The local hawkers were there too, selling figs and nuts; dogs ran about in the forest of legs, and emitted piercing yelps if and when trodden upon; beggars accosted all and sundry for alms, while picturesquely

dressed men and boys lounged about looking on with
the greatest interest at the new-comers. They had
never seen British troops before, and our kilts caused
them considerable amusement in addition to the usual
curiosity. Near the fountain was a pretentious building used as a hospital. The medical staff and
patients, including some captured British soldiers,
still remained, guards being placed over the building.
On a balcony were two German doctors and a nurse
contemplating the animated scene at the fountain, and
in casting them a glance I could not help wondering
what was passing in their minds. But we had no
time for them or their thoughts, for we were in search
of treasure. We left the busy scene, and investigated
the narrow streets and alley-ways that appeared to
the inexperienced eye capable of harbouring the worst
of bad characters, and the darkest of dark deeds,
whilst the hovels on either side might have been dens
of infamy. This, of course, is the judgment one would
undoubtedly arrive at had one come across such a
place in Europe, but in the wilds of Gilead things are
different. So without entertaining any fears we continued our search, traversing a maze of narrow alleys
until, turning a corner, we knew the treasure of our
quest was near. We could smell it. Passing through
a low opening in a wall we entered a dark apartment
with no other means of access for light or air than
the entrance. The walls were black with grime and
age, and it required some seconds to get accustomed
to the gloom. In one corner was a long mud-built
oven, and a fire burning just inside the mouth threw
a faint red glow on a native busily engaged over a
large flat pan. This was the baker's shop and the
native, the baker. Pressing against a large slab of
rock serving as a counter was a motley crowd of native

women and children, eager to buy bread or to have small portions of goat flesh cooked in the oven. The baker rolled out the dough in flat pancakes the size of a large tea plate, placed them one by one on a long-handled wooden spade, and tossed them to the far end of the oven. At our entry he looked up with apprehension, but on our intimating that we were there for the purpose of peaceful trading he was reassured and proceeded with his work. In due course a number of flat pancakes of unleavened bread were assigned to us, for which we paid and took our departure, much to the relief, I believe, of the women and children, who held us somewhat in awe.

As we made our way back to camp, through the outskirts of the town, a great commotion was created by crowds of natives outside what had evidently been a new stone building of European architecture. It appeared that the people of Es Salt, or a section of them, probably the Armenians, engendering no feelings of friendship towards the Turks, had demonstrated their aversion by firing upon them as they took their departure the previous night. This building had been the Ottoman Headquarters, and no time had been lost by the mob in helping themselves to anything and everything of value. They had stripped the building bare, even of the roof and all woodwork, leaving only the walls standing. Men, women, and children were shouting and yelling, quarrelling and fighting amongst themselves over the loot, and every now and then the livelier spirits fired their rifles to add to the general pandemonium. In a community where such a state of affairs can exist, the law of "might is right" is the only one recognized, the strongest secure everything worth having, whilst the weaker ones go without; and if by chance they do win a prize it is soon wrested from them.

That afternoon we shifted camp to a more convenient spot in the shelter of a large re-entrant where the majority of the other camps were situated. Early the next morning, as soon as everyone was astir, an aeroplane swooped down out of the clouds, and after hovering for an instant like a hawk about to pounce upon its prey, the engine re-started with a loud roar, and the machine made off. The suddenness of its appearance took us completely by surprise, and before action could be taken it was away and out of range, for we had no anti-aircraft guns. The tactics adopted, quite apart from identification marks, clearly showed that it was an enemy machine. Orders were immediately issued to prepare against its return. Lewis guns were brought from their panniers and magazines fixed, machine guns mounted on tripods, and ammunition belts slipped in the breeches, whilst every rifle in the Brigade was loaded and held in readiness. Surely enough, in a few minutes, the stentorian growl of the engines was heard, and over a neighbouring ridge, travelling at a terrific rate, the foe appeared. Straight for our re-entrant it flew, descending as it approached. Nearer and nearer and still lower it came, when suddenly from every square yard of the re-entrant burst a perfect hail of lead from machine guns, Lewis guns and rifles, all aimed at the one target. With every second the range decreased, and with every second the firing increased, till there was such a deafening noise that the roar of the engines was completely nullified, and it was impossible to hear oneself shout. And still the machine flew on. Passing right over our heads it turned, rose, then circled round, dived and turned again, and was off towards the Jordan. The absence of any bombing on the part of the aeroplane rather suggested that the object of the visit was purely observation, combined, perhaps, with the taking of photographs. If the latter, then it is reasonable to assume that by the daring and persistency of the pilot many valuable views were obtained, but they never reached Turkish hands. Some distance down the Es Salt road the machine was forced to come down near a Royal Engineers' dump, undoubtedly in consequence of our fire, so that although many thousands of rounds were expended they were by no means wasted. It is extremely difficult to bring an aeroplane down by rifle or machine gun fire, for although it may be hit a dozen times, it is not rendered *hors de combat* until some vital part has been injured.

The military situation now emerged from the pall of obscurity behind which it had seemed to us to be hidden, and a scheme of defence was decided upon and adopted. Two Battalions, the "15th" and "16th," formed a line on the hills to the north of Es Salt with the right flank swinging round to the north-east, whilst a detachment of cavalry protected the town from the west and north-west. Passing as it did through a wild and hostile country our line of communication was of too great a length to be left without some protection midway. Accordingly, our Battalion and the "13th" were ordered to proceed to El Howeij, a spot some six miles down the road where the Turks had recently constructed a stone bridge spanning the wady. It was a fine morning, and as we left the town the major portion of the inhabitants turned out to see our departure. The descent to the road was so rocky and broken that we soon developed into a disorganized mob, but forming up at the bottom we set off in column of route, with the pipers and drummers leading. Away up on the hillside the roofs of the houses were packed with people and the roadway itself was lined on either side with Bedouins, Arabs, Armenians, beggars, waifs and strays, and goodness knows how many other species of mankind, all gathered together to witness the wonderful sight of a kilted regiment on the march. Never before in the history of Gilead had such a spectacle occurred to demand the cessation of all pursuits. It was more like an occasion for a Bank Holiday, except that in Es Salt such institutions are unknown, every man being the custodian of his own wealth. At the corner where the road takes a sharp turn an official photographer was getting his kinematic camera in position with swarms of young Es Saltonians around him gaping in wide-eyed wonderment. But when the order was given to " Quick-*march !* " the drums gave a warning roll, captured Turkish drums to boot, the pipes commenced to skirl, and the delight of the natives soared to the highest pitch. The poor photographer, reeling off dozens of yards of film in immortalizing the occasion, was immediately forsaken. His mysterious box on three sticks no longer had any interest for the native mind, and as we marched, a multitude of men and boys pushed and scrambled for places alongside the pipers, succumbing to the charm of the music like iron filing to the attractions of a magnet. The bagpipes make an irresistible appeal to the Arabs, even eclipsing that of the young martial spirits of Britain upon the approach of a military band. The natives rushed forward frantically until they met the object of their fascination, when they attached themselves to it with childish delight. For two or three miles they kept up with us, falling off now and then in little groups, until eventually we were unaccompanied except for the echoes that danced among the rocks on the hillside and scampered with delight and merriment up the valleys until swallowed up in the fastnesses of some rugged gorge.

We reached our destination soon after noon, and camped a little way up the slopes of the hills overlooking the road and the brand new bridge which the Turks, through no fault of their own, had left undamaged. That afternoon and the following day were spent in bathing and washing clothes in the rushing waters of the wady that runs alongside the road, a measure the necessity for which was equalled only by our appreciation. Besides these cleansing operations, neat roadways were made through and around the camp, obstructing bushes and trees cut down, and to judge by the fanciful town-planning scheme laboriously worked out by certain people with nothing more practical to occupy their minds, a prolonged stay there of at least six months was contemplated.

That evening the camp was a picture of peacefulness. Every little bivouac had its small glimmer of light from some treasured stump of candle, or improvised lamp composed of a tin of rifle oil and a piece of string for a wick, and the low murmuring of voices rose on the still air like the hum of many bees. The troops were engaged upon a variety of occupations; some gathered together and chatted over past happenings or formed great plans for when they would get home—many of them, alas, never lived to realize their hopes—others sat quietly with book and pipe, while the more thoughtful, perhaps, seized the opportunity of writing a letter home ready for the collection of the next mail, reading and re-reading a

THE 2ND BATTALION LONDON SCOTTISH LEAVING ES SALT, MARCH 27TH, 1918.

Photograph from Regimental Gazette.

much crumpled epistle, the last received from some far-away correspondent and written months previously. An atmosphere of tranquillity pervaded the whole scene, and would easily have given the lie to a statement that this was in the heart of an enemy country, and that a horde of Turks might even then have been lurking in the neighbourhood. Beds were laid and everyone prepared to turn in for a good night's sleep. " Orderly " sergeants were summoned to receive the orders for the morrow, and one or two men expressed the feeling that everything was too comfortable to last long, asserting that " something's in the wind." They were immediately admonished for their chronic pessimism. But hark! What was that? " Pack up . . . form . . . road . . . move off . . . rations and water." Such fragments of speech were suddenly heard a little distance off, and then the Sergeant-Major's voice rang out with orders for those in charge of pack animals. Uneasy glances were exchanged in the bivouacs, and all strained every nerve to catch the indistinct orders. Presently the platoon sergeants came round with definite information. An urgent call had come from Es Salt and we were to proceed thither without delay. Rations were issued in great haste, but each man received his just portion, water-bottles filled, bivouacs struck and everything packed. The animals were loaded, and in less than an hour the peaceful camp had disappeared, and the Battalion was formed up on the road ready to move off.

The Turks at Amman would by this time have been fully occupied with the nucleus of our raiding force, so that it was unlikely the cause of the alarm had come from that quarter. Alternatively, the enemy had massed a considerable force to the north of Es

Salt, and was threatening our defensive positions. The latter proved to be the case.

We reached the town in the small hours of morning after a forced march, and found everything quiet and still. Passing through the silent and deserted streets we mounted the hill by a rough track and halted at the Headquarters of the 15th Battalion. Two Companies were sent forward in support, while the remainder stayed where they were until dawn. The Commanding Officer of the " 15th " being home on leave, the Major was in command of the Battalion, and there seemed to be some uncertainty and not a little uneasiness as to what was the exact position of things. A conference was held, whereupon our Colonel, elucidating the position, took command of the two Battalions, and so great was the faith of the whole Brigade in him, that general relief was felt on this step being taken.

As soon as it was light enough to see the nature of the ground, we moved farther forward in a supporting position and established Battalion Headquarters at a convenient place. Our positions were situated on the summit of Jebel Osha, a composite height of Mount Gilead, or, as the Arabs call it, " Jebel Jelaad." A force of about two thousand Turks was occupying a line on a ridge of three hills to the north-west, and as strong reinforcements were on the way, was expected to try and break through to regain possession of Es Salt. We would not have given much for its chances of success, but still, it was a contingency that had to be reckoned with.

Before very long I received instructions to compile a map of our positions, also showing approximately those of the enemy. Fortunately the old maps had been revised, and a prominent point

called Kefr Huda had been fixed trigonometrically.
Es Salt itself had been shifted two miles farther north
in these revisions, but by means of back bearings on
Kefr Huda and cross bearings from a prominent
mound in the town, triangulation of sufficient accuracy
for our purpose was obtained. I was shown round the
line by the Intelligence Officer of the "15th," in order
that my map might show the exact disposition of the
front-line troops. This officer led the way over a
saddle, which he assured me was not under observation
by the enemy. The ground was extremely stony, and
in places strewn with huge boulders. We had not
proceeded very far when suddenly a number of shots
were fired at us from a hill to the west, which had
hitherto been considered unoccupied. The firing
rapidly increased until it seemed we were the object
of great excitement amongst the enemy. Bullets were
striking the rocks all around us and whizzing over
our heads, but thanks be to the poor shooting of the
Turks, or to Providence, neither of us was hit. My
companion deemed it wise to make a bolt for some
dead ground, which he reached in safety, so I
decided to drop flat behind a heap of stones in order
to divide the enemy's attention. The firing continued
for some minutes, the spiteful missiles striking the
stones in front and all round. After an interval I
deemed it safe to make a move. It would have been
fatal to have reappeared at the spot where I was last
seen, so crawling along for some yards I suddenly
jumped to my feet and ran for dear life towards the
dead ground. The old trick succeeded, for though
the Turks wasted more shots, before they could align
their sights, I was safe. The incident was not without
its value, for we were able definitely to locate the
enemy, and my map benefited to that extent.

Whilst we were at Es Salt a band of about two hundred natives from the town came to the camp, each armed to the teeth with a rifle, two or three murderous-looking knives thrust in their sashes, and machine gun belts, filled with ammunition, wound round their bodies in the approved fashion of the day. They were commanded by a Sheikh, or head-tribesman. Stopping their straggling procession outside the cave serving as Battalion Headquarters, they made representations to the Colonel of their desire to help us with our war, and permission was asked to be allowed to take an active part. A more bloodthirsty mob it would be difficult to find, but it must be said in their favour that they were imbued with an exuberance of enthusiasm for our cause, quite unexpected from such a source, not unmingled, perhaps, with a spark of self-interest. These were the gentry who had been instrumental in accelerating the Turks' departure from the town, the anticipation of whose revenge, if they ever returned, would account for the present concern of the natives. Hence their desire to help us!

In proof of their prowess they fired shot after shot over the hills in the direction of the enemy, and, laughing gleefully, they would come close and confide to us that " Turk maffeesh," meaning that the Turkish *regime* was at an end and the triumph of British arms assured. No doubt the wish was father to the thought. However, so long as they remained in that frame of mind, and supplied their own ammunition, they could do no harm. As it was judicious to humour them, this noble band of cut-throats was conducted to a hill in the front line, well clear of our own troops, where they were told to take cover behind a circular stone wall, similar to those built by shepherds, which was

thenceforth known as "Dagoes' Redoubt." They
were then entirely in their element, and crouched low
behind the breastwork, to carry out their self-imposed
duty to King George—and themselves.

The procedure adopted by these amateur warriors
was decidedly humorous. At one end of the redoubt
a sentry was posted to keep watch upon the doings of
"John Turk." Not satisfied with the trust reposed in
the watcher, or lacking in confidence in the clearness
of his vision, each brave could not resist the temptation
to have a look for himself, with the result that there
was such a bobbing up of heads over the top of the
wall that it was enough to make a good scout gnash
his teeth. Eventually the lynx-eyed merchant at the
end saw something moving out in front, or thought he
did, and communicated the fact to the chief by
standing up full-length, pointing excitedly, with
outstretched arms, and shouting at the top of his voice.
At this there was a great commotion. The Sheikh
gave an order, and two hundred rifles were levelled
over the wall; another order, and two hundred shots
rang out, fired in as many directions. By the exultant
joy which followed, anyone would have thought that
they had slain half the Turkish Army, and it was some
minutes before they again subsided into a state of
composure. Far from doing harm, this practice was
likely to impress the enemy, however wrongly, with
our superiority in numbers and the vigilance of
our observation. The dagoes were, therefore, not
interfered with, and were allowed to enjoy themselves
to the full. The limit of their enjoyment though, was
reached each day at dusk. Evidently not wishing to
run the risk of a nervous breakdown, they withdrew
at the very time when an attack might have taken
place, and sought the seclusion and safety of their

own homes; no doubt afterwards relating in glowing terms to their fellow-townsmen with what valour they had kept off the threatening foe. But they would turn up to business again in the morning, all smiles and cartridge belts, to spend another nerve-racking day in " Dagoes' Redoubt."

The 16th Battalion on the right had a similar experience. They, however, derived some material benefit from the escapades of a young Armenian, who, with half a dozen daring spirits from the town, used to go out and raid the Turkish posts, invariably bringing back prisoners. Handing over the captives to the troops, he and his band would go off again on some fresh adventure, returning as successfully as before.

That all-important factor, the weather, which regulates our tempers and determines our happiness, which dominates our spirits by raising our hopes or reducing us to utter despondency, again visited upon us one of its most inclement moods, to play upon our susceptibilities, banish cheerfulness, and to create a gloomy outlook on life generally. It rained, it blew half a gale, and was very cold. Everybody was miserable. Half a dozen of us, all scouts, had bivouacked together, and when not engaged upon our various duties, sang in chorus (harmonizing where we could) fragments of comic opera, hymns, or the latest songs (two years old)—anything to forget our wretchedness!

Fortunately our supplies were regular, and though by no means magnificent, were plenteous. One day, in support of the axiom that " wonders will never cease " to astonish mortal man, a bag of letters arrived with the Battalion's rations. A mail, however small and however long overdue, always marks a red-letter day, especially when you are in the heart of a strange land and have nothing but your own optimism to make life worth living. On the arrival of the mail the news travelled round like the wind, and everyone was filled with eager expectation. Volunteers were not lacking to carry it from the dump, and the pipers, whose duty it was to sort it, needed no exhortation to use expedition. To those of us who received these links with home, the letters acted for some days as a stimulant, and provided food for thought and sweet recollections; but for the unfortunates who did not, disappointment and despondency was all *they* got from the mail. I have known men not to receive a letter for months on end, owing to the continual loss of mails at sea or other causes, and they have become so depressed and miserable that they were entirely indifferent as to whether they survived the war or not. They felt absolutely forgotten, and the total absence of any possibility of leave home, coupled with the uncertainty as to how long they were to be " buried alive," often caused them to sink into such a deplorable state of apathy and neglect of their personal cleanliness that in time they fell sick and had to go to hospital. There the change of environment and decent food generally restored their health and nursed them back to a normal state of mind.

Adversities never come singly. The attack by the Turks was expected during the night against the " 15th " (whom we were supporting), and of course the weather was at its worst. It was quite probable that the enemy had received reinforcements, but this notwithstanding, they were to be repulsed at all costs. Never could we allow them to break through, and cut off the retreat of the Amman force! Accordingly, the line was strengthened, supports and reserves moved close up at dusk, and additional posts were established where necessary or expedient. A field battery of artillery and a howitzer gun had arrived to give us that material support which has such wonderful moral effect on either attacking or defending troops. In due course the advance of the Turks was heralded by rifle fire and a few shells. Very few casualties were reported, and the attack proved to be but a half-hearted effort. In one instance a party of the enemy succeeded in approaching to within a few yards of one of the machine gun posts, but they were detected in time, and few of them got back. The " 15th " held their ground everywhere and the attack fizzled out.

The force advancing against Amman was greatly hampered by the difficult country. Transport was necessarily slow, owing to the bad state of the road, made worse by the recent rain. The motto, " Keep your baccy dry and trust to the artillery," did not hold good out here, for it was impossible to get the guns along. The New Zealanders reached the railway south of Amman, and commenced the work of demolition, but the tunnel, the chief object of destruction, could not be reached. An Infantry Brigade arrived from Es Salt on March 28th, and co-operating with the Australians, attacked the town from the north. Little progress was made, the Turks counter-attacking again and again. Reinforcements were sent, and the attack renewed, but still the enemy maintained his ground. The country was extremely wild, and favoured the Turkish snipers, who are past-masters in the art. News was then received that a large body of Turkish troops was marching on Es Salt, and as we had no reinforcements available to strengthen our garrison a withdrawal was ordered.

After inflicting as much damage to the railway as

possible, including the destruction of several bridges, the Amman force retired. Our Brigade was to hold on until the force had passed through Es Salt and was well on the way back to the Jordan, and then to retire by way of the road with the exception of our Battalion, which, having relieved the " 15th " in the line, would be the last to withdraw and would return by the Arseniyet Track.

On April 1st all sick and wounded were evacuated and all camel transport proceeded by the road early in the morning. The utmost secrecy was observed, for with the continual coming and going of the natives, many of whom could not be trusted, communication with the enemy would have been a simple matter. It was not possible, though, to conceal the clearing of the hospital and removal of stores, which operations the inhabitants were quick to connect with some impending move on our part. Our band of braves failed to put in an appearance that day, but lounged at their doorways scowling at passing troops, or gathered about the town in knots engaged in earnest conversation. At the approach of any of our men their voices would be lowered and their sullen looks spelt suspicion and a departed faith. All through the day parties of Armenians packed up their belongings, gathered together their goats and fowls, and set off down the road to the Jordan, preferring to leave their homes as refugees than risk the retaliation of the Turks when they returned.

As soon as darkness fell we packed our kit and waited for the order to move. A little way along the Amman road a bright glare emanated from a number of captured Turkish motor-lorries, which were so embedded in the mud that it was impossible to move them, so they were burned. When the reflection died down, the darkness became intense. A peculiar excitement had taken hold of us as we sat about and waited; the silence was strained and awesome. All of a sudden a gun roared out, and for a moment set us all wondering what had happened. But it was one of our own faithful friends sending an occasional shell over to the Turks before departing, just to let them know that we were still there, and had no intention whatever of going.

At about ten o'clock the order came. A roll was called in muffled whispers and every man accounted for. The front-line platoons quietly left their positions and joined the main body. The officers, or platoon sergeants where there were no officers, reported " all present " to the Adjutant and we set off into the night. Cautiously picking our way through the inky blackness, and fearful lest the Turks should hear the scraping of our nailed boots on the stones, we pressed on, anxious to increase our distance from the place as rapidly as possible. If the enemy had taken it into his head to attack just then, the result would have been little short of catastrophic. In single file we trudged on, stumbling over boulders, catching our feet in vines, all the time living in dread of making a noise or losing sight of the dim figure of the man in front. With every yard we gained confidence. The exigencies of the occasion were a sufficient incentive to urge us on, and in spite of the difficulties of the ground we made fair progress.

With the rising of the moon shortly after midnight the sky cleared and we were more or less able to see where we were going, though for the first hour or so the wadies were in shadow. With the descent from the bleak heights of Gilead the air became noticeably warmer, and this change must have had a slumberous effect upon us, for in no other way can the sudden sleepiness with which we were overcome be accounted for. The hourly halts were observed, and no sooner did some men sit or lie down than their heads began to nod, and unable to resist the allurements of Morpheus, they dozed off to sleep.

The commotion of putting on equipment again roused them, and rising up, they would follow suit, walking on mechanically, quite oblivious as to where they were or whither they were going. As hour after hour passed, the fatigue of the march acted as a contributory cause to the general drowsiness; but there was no stopping. On and on we went, mile after mile, always descending, sometimes climbing down steep, narrow goat tracks, at other times making up for lost time on a broad gradual descent. Men actually slept on the march. When, as frequently happened, a check came, the senses of some were beyond noticing it, and they went crashing into the pack of the man in front. Pulling up with a start, they would stare wildly round in a fitful wakefulness, and again subside into a state of unconsciousness. In a minute or two the column would move on, but these poor fellows still stood there, with their chins resting on their chests, fast asleep. The man behind being more wakeful, would give the sleeper a push, whereupon he would start up, realize that there was a stretch of empty pathway in front of him, and set off in fevered haste to catch up. These irregular spurts continually occurred, making it very trying for those in rear to keep in touch, for with every yard lost in front, a dozen had to be made up by the time the check had reached the tail of the column.

The approach of dawn found us amongst the foothills bordering on the plain. At this stage the withdrawal could be considered an accomplished fact, so a halt of an hour was made, during which we were to sleep.   Loads were taken off the pack animals, men rolled themselves in bivouac sheets, and sentries were posted in short reliefs to keep watch over the sleeping Battalion.   Little did we then know that the Turks were following us but three hours behind! Promptly at the expiration of an hour the sentries roused the camp, and in five minutes the long column was trailing through the pass with renewed energy, for the brief spell had worked wonders.   At break of day we emerged on to the plain and there met our ration convoy.   Halting for the purpose, rations and water were issued, and short though the time was, innumerable little fires were lighted with dried grass, over which innumerable mess-tins of water were soon boiling to make tea, the refreshing beverage upon which we were forced to rely so much.

At this juncture a low droning was heard in the heavens, and a swarm of some dozen aeroplanes appeared from the north.   The whole Battalion scattered, rifles were loaded, and we waited for an opportunity to welcome them with a shower of bullets. Whether the news of their ill-fated brother at Es Salt acted as a deterrent or no, it is hard to say, but strangely enough, no sooner had we made this preparation than the machines separated and flew in different directions.   Again converging farther south, these aeronautic marauders dropped bombs on a party of cavalry which was crossing the plain, but happily no damage was done, and they flew over the Jordan in search of further prey.

In about two hours we reached Ghoraniyeh, and splashing through the swift running waters of the Nimrin, not caring how wet we got in the process, we reached the bridge. Once on the western side a lengthy halt was made. We were too worn out to eat, so dragging off our wet things we spread them out in the hot sun to dry, and taking advantage of any small patch of shade to shelter our heads, fell asleep.

In sixteen hours we had traversed twenty-four miles of the most wild and rugged country, and experienced a violent change in climate varying from the piercing blasts of the Mountains of Gilead to the sweltering plains of Jericho. In the cool of the evening we continued our journey, and eventually camped among the prickly Spina Christi bushes a stone's throw from Jericho.

Just by the bridge on the eastern bank of the Jordan was a huge pile of rifles which had been taken from the refugees—for it would have been ill-advised to allow them to retain their weapons once they had crossed—a heterogeneous collection of fire-arms well qualified for a place in any museum.

P

CHAPTER XX

RELIEVED of the anxieties and strain of the previous twenty-four hours, and knowing that our work was finished with all danger past, we lapsed into a state of complete mental and physical lassitude, and readily yielding to the dictates of Nature, lay down that night to enjoy one of the sweetest of Nature's gifts, a sound, dreamless sleep. So utterly worn out were we, and so soundly did we sleep, that it is difficult to say how far the day would have advanced before we roused ourselves if an anti-aircraft gun, tucked away in the outskirts of Jericho, had not raised its voice in vehement protest at the continuance of a certain loud, humming noise. "Silence!" it seemed to command, "how dare you disturb the slumbers of these trusty warriors? Be off with you, and cultivate a little more delicacy of feeling!" But not the slightest notice was taken. The sun was already well on its journey across the heavens and penetrated the bivouacs with sharp, burning rays. Voices began to murmur, heads were thrust out between the buttoned sheets, and eyes searched the blue expanse for the perpetrators of this fresh outrage. The little gun again roared out in authoritative tones, and expectorated little flaky balls of white smoke at two enemy aeroplanes that were hovering about overhead, their white wings glistening as they caught the light of the sun. But it was of no avail, they refused to go. The balls of smoke floated pleasantly away upon the light breeze, and dissolved; the little gun ceased its barking, and presently, up soared a smart scout machine, the very acme of speed and cunning, gurgling and snorting with indignation at the effrontery of the two interlopers. Higher and higher it mounted into the heavens until it appeared to be above its opponents. After circling round two or three times, it swooped down at tremendous speed, making straight for one of them, so that a collision seemed inevitable. But the parallax was deceiving. The sharp " pop-pop " of a Lewis gun was heard and the scout raced past the other, pumping lead as hard as it could go. The third machine, hoping to gain the ascendency over the solitary foe, rose higher and endeavoured to fire on it from above. The little machine with the tri-coloured rings was on the alert, however, and anticipating the tactic, dived and twisted, raced hither and thither, darted first at one, just missed, turned, and directed its attention to the other, first on top, then underneath, performing such acrobatic feats of a hair-raising nature, firing all the time, that the pilots of the hostile machines could not possibly have known for many seconds together where they were, nor the whereabouts of their mobile adversary. Under these circumstances the conclusion that the Devil himself had taken to a pair of wings in order to indulge in a little aeronautic playfulness would have been quite justifiable, and these thoughts may have passed through the minds of the enemy, for in a very short time they tired of the contest, and seizing the first opportunity that came along, made off towards their own territory.

No routine was arranged for that day and we were permitted to disport ourselves according to fancy.

the darkness, quicker and quicker as the incentive took hold of each man to hurry on to the foothills and get some sort of cover. What mattered if the Turks were there? It would be a straight fight. The flashes broke out afresh accompanied by the monotonous knocking sound of the machine guns. Stepping reverently over a dead form here, and closing up a gap there, each man trusted to God to see him through. When you are face to face with death like this peculiar thoughts flash through your mind, and you realize that each one of them may be your last.

At dawn the hills were reached, and by a tremendous effort we captured the enemy's first line of defence and gained a footing on them, but only a footing, and at heavy cost. All the higher positions dominating our own were strongly occupied by the enemy, of whom there appeared to be thousands. By some unknown means they had dragged mountain and small field guns up there, with which they fired at us continually, while every hill-top and ridge seemed to bristle with machine guns.

It was fatal to expose yourself, for as sure as you did a bullet would come whizzing past your ear, or perhaps would not pass at all.

The Battalion on our right had come to a standstill, so having got so far, it was impossible for us to get farther without exposing our flank. Every piece of cover was used to its fullest advantage, and we simply had to lie still and await developments.

All that morning a continual procession of wounded men made their way back to the dressing station, some light hearted in spite of their wounds, others trying to be; some limping along unaided and making good progress, others lying painfully upon stretchers,

assistant, but one entrusted with the deepest of deep
secrets, and the most precious of maps, in short, the
welfare of the whole Battalion. For purposes of
transport it was allotted the whole side of a mule, and
to prove the status it held, it fraternized with the
C.O.'s personal kit which was carried on the other
side. As for the mule saddled with the great responsibility of carrying these treasures, his nescience being
of the average amongst mules, the close proximity to
his poor fuddled brain of so much knowledge must
have given him brain fever, for after a time he was
sent to an equine health resort down the line for three
months' grazing to recuperate. But after all, perhaps,
the brute was overcome by the avoirdupois on the
Colonel's side of him, for such was the weight
and extent of the C.O.'s baggage, that a couple
of camels besides this half mule were necessary to
transport it.

Whilst on the subject of mules, it must be said
that our supply of these invaluable animals was
excellent. Many of them were as big as an average-
sized horse, though far more useful, for wherever a
man could go in the rocky country we had to negotiate,
the mules could go too. I have seen them climb
down six feet terrace walls. Of course they damaged
the walls, but they got down safely with their loads.
As for eating, well, the muleteers could discourse at
length upon their propensities in that direction, the
condition of whose clothing and equipment would bear
out most of their statements. But I will not waste
time eulogizing these animals, for their peculiar
qualities are well known; if anyone is thirsting for
further knowledge on the subject, I should advise him
to seize the first opportunity of becoming a muleteer,
a capacity which is an incorporation of guide,

philosopher, friend, task-master, nurse and administrator of condign punishment all rolled into one.

During the raid several enemy mules fell into our hands; enemy mules in so far as they served the Turks, but a square meal soon made them *our* faithful servants. They were of a much inferior breed to our own, small, skinny and generally bearing signs of bad treatment in the form of cuts and open sores caused by chafing. Again making a comparison, these beasts were infinitely superior to those owned by the natives, which were under-sized, under-fed, but very much over-worked. Small wonder, then, that they never seemed to grow or clothe their stunted frames with any better covering than a scarred, dirty, moth-eaten looking skin. Their camels similarly were poor specimens of their kind. They were the last word in scragginess and would have made excellent studies in osteology.

Our mules were always objects of covetous glances from the Bedouins, even surpassing their insatiable desire to possess some of our blankets. British army blankets were particularly attractive to these people, owing to their great superiority to the coarse blanket cloth with which the Bedouins construct their bivouacs. There was a Bedouin encampment near Jericho, and we found the men-folk were continually lurking round our camp to see whether they could steal any of our best Witneys, or anything else for that matter, but a strict watch was kept. Knowing them to be inveterate thieves, they were generally driven off and threatened with all kinds of terrible punishment if they dared return.

It is difficult to tell how these nomads live if it is not by robbery, for they do not stay in any one place long enough to cultivate the land, and except for keeping a few goats and fowls they have no visible means of subsistence. Their live-stock, babies, and utensils are all mixed up together in their tents, and as you stroll by, your nostrils are assailed by unpleasant odours, and your ears are smitten by a cacophonous chorus of bleats, cackles and infantile yells, tempered at every few bars by the interposition of a harsh parental voice by way of admonishment for the breach created in the domestic peace and quiet.

After two days at Jericho we set off to march back to Jerusalem. When not actually engaged in operations we always seemed to be marching either back to Jerusalem or setting out from Jerusalem upon some fresh expedition. We made the journey along the Jericho road about six times in all, and whether by day or by night every one of the fifteen miles became painfully familiar. On this occasion we camped at Talat ed Dumm.

Whilst here I took a stroll over the neighbouring hills armed with my sketch-book in the hope that the ancient Crusaders' Castle would prove material for a sketch, but the view was poor and of no value. I was about to return to camp when I noticed a native lurking not far away, evidently contemplating flight. I shouted to him and motioned him to approach, which he did with ostensible reluctance. On coming up he stood with eyes downcast and seemed as if he expected to be taken prisoner or ill-treated. He was of middle age, very ragged, dirty, and very frightened. I imagined that he belonged to one of the nomadic families which had been hiding in the caves of the neighbourhood during the Turkish occupation. "Here is an opportunity," I thought, "of sketching from the raw material." I showed him my sketch-book and intimated by signs that he would please me by squatting down for a few minutes whilst I committed his dirty face to clean paper. But he did not understand, and stood there staring at me with a hunted look in his eyes, muttering. I thought I could diagnose his complaint, however, so searching in my haversack I found a very ancient piece of biscuit which I handed to him. Greedily snatching it from me he began to devour it ravenously, as though he had not had anything to eat for a week. I made him sit down and commenced to sketch, but his fidgetiness made it very difficult. He crunched away at his biscuit with great enthusiasm, whilst I sketched. As long as the inducement lasted I was sure of my model, but no sooner had he finished the last precious crumb, than he jumped up and unceremoniously fled down the hill leaving me to stare after him in utter amazement with a half-finished sketch.

Continuing the next day we passed through Jerusalem and again camped at Shafat. Nobody seemed to know quite where we were going or what was expected of us, but that there was more marching to do was certain. Since Christmas our services had been divided between the line astride the Nablus road in the north, and the Jordan Valley in the east, entailing long and tiring marches to and fro. Whilst we were exploring the wilds of Gilead, the troops holding the line in the Nablus sector had advanced several thousand yards. It transpired, whilst we were at Shafat, that our Brigade was to proceed to Jiljillia, a village a mile to the west of the Nablus road, and relieve a Brigade of the 10th (Irish) Division which was to co-operate in a raid farther west.

We were now well advanced into the month of April. The weather had generally improved, and the hills were covered once more with prolific vegetation, providing a refreshing sight from the barren sameness of the Jericho Plain. The hot sun also went to show that the summer was upon us. It was the height of the orange season, and at every halting place our camp was besieged by a small army of natives with sacks and baskets filled with luscious fruit from the groves around Jaffa and Ludd. Realizing the medicinal value of oranges, the authorities encouraged the native vendors, allotting them a specified area, where a market was established. The fruit was the largest I have ever seen, and the usual price was three for two piastres, or just under twopence each. Many a time four comrades and myself have commenced the day with fifty or sixty oranges, and by night none remained. It is to be feared that our liking for the fruit developed into a gluttony, though happily, no harm came of our excesses.

On the third day of the march, we reached the great Wady el Jibb, a deep, rugged gorge, which harboured the stores and general supplies of the units holding the line. The sides of the wady rose to some four or five hundred feet, on the northern heights of which were the British positions.

The country hereabouts and farther north around Nablus, the ancient Shechem, is teeming with Biblical associations, is very fertile, and, but for its mountainous nature, would be as productive as the neighbourhood around Bethlehem.

From our camp in the Wady el Jibb the Scout Sergeant and I went on twelve hours ahead to "take over" from the Irish "Intelligence" officer. We were hospitably received and obtained full information concerning the Battalion frontage, but of maps there were none. The following morning the relief was effected and we settled down to the usual routine.

Fresh observation posts were made, and needless to say, a contour map was required showing every post and sangar and the approaches thereto. In about a week, as soon as the map had attained a state as near perfection as possible, the Irishmen returned, and so got the benefit of my labours.

This was quite a usual state of affairs. As a rule when we took over a section of the line, we had next to nothing handed over in the way of maps or information, and as soon as we had made an elaborate map, located the enemy's posts and improved our own, we were relieved. It seemed almost as though this was our special vocation. However, having completed our job the line was handed over to the Irish again, whereupon we withdrew and retraced our steps to Jerusalem.

The weather was now very hot, so we rested during the day and marched by night. On the third night we occupied our old camping ground at Shafat. Up till then it was unknown what our next task was to be. Many rumours went floating around, including the staid old chestnut that we were going for a rest. How true that prediction was will be seen in due course. For many, alas, it *was* a rest, and a long one; but of that we must treat in its proper place.

CHAPTER XXI

THE Jordan was to be crossed again and our Division
(less one Brigade) was to attack the enemy's positions,
Shunet Nimrin—El Haud, and destroy the force,
numbering about five thousand, holding those
positions. The cavalry were to work through the
hills, capture Es Salt, and hold the town until
the Hedjaz Arabs could advance and relieve them.

At the close of a gorgeous day we struck camp and
set out upon our second expedition across the famous
river. As we marched along the ridge of the Mount
of Olives the setting sun was throwing his red glow
over the Holy City, and to the east the foothills of
that wall of mountains across the Jordan reposed
behind a veneer of soft mauve and blue, calm and
beautiful. Yet in a very short time their peace would
be shattered, the roar and din of battle would echo and
re-echo amongst the mountain fastnesses, the rugged
defiles and narrow gorges now shrouded in evening
gloom. Under their shadow many a high-spirited
fellow whose gaze wandered now carelessly, now
admiringly, in their direction as he marched along,
would lie in his grave. Through the village of
Et Tor we passed, and round the sweeping curves
through Bethany, the sound of the bagpipes bringing
crowds of villagers hurrying to the roadside to see us

235

pass, and our ever mechanical step stirring up clouds of white dust, smothering them in it.   Then round the sharp hairpin bends as the road descends abruptly from the Mount and finally reaching the lower road, we settled down to cover the monotonous miles as best we could.

Thanks be to our pipers and drummers we derived considerable stimulation from their music during long marches.   The third and fourth hours of a march are by far the worst, and you feel as though you can hardly drag one weary leg after the other.   Your back begins to bend beneath the weight of your pack, and the step changes every other minute.   The periodical halts seem a terribly long time in coming, and you are convinced that the Colonel's watch has stopped, and that you have already marched half an hour overtime. Then a preliminary roll of drums travels down the column, and the pipes burst forth once again to help you on your weary way.   The effect is wonderful. Your back, and the back of your neighbour, in fact everyone's back, immediately straightens; shoulders are squared, and the step again goes with a swing as though each man is anxious to convey to his fellow sufferers that he is not at all tired, but, on the contrary, quite fresh.   In ten minutes the unwelcome double beat of the drums is heard, one more round, and the music stops.   The rhythm of the step again falls to pieces, backs begin to droop, heads drop lower, and chins rest on chests in the struggle with the strain on endurance.   At length the welcome halt comes, and then for ten minutes you lie prone on your back in glorious relaxation, contemplating the heavens and feebly blinking at the bright moon.

Breaking our journey at Talat ed Dumm we continued the next night descending to the plain, passing through Jericho and following the road to Ghoraniyeh. It was a very tedious march, much longer than that of the previous night, and we were all dog-tired long before we reached the river. A wooden suspension bridge had been constructed since we were last there, and crossing by this we secluded ourselves amongst the dense bush and scrub on the eastern bank where we lay down to sleep for the few remaining hours till dawn.

It seemed we had hardly dropped off to sleep when the sun rose. Very soon his scorching rays forced us to put up bivouacs, inside which we sweltered all day, tormented by millions of flies and clouds of mosquitoes. We were unable to light fires to cook anything, and dared not walk about outside as we were under observation. All day I was busy marking on the Battalion maps the positions of fresh enemy posts and guns.

In the evening we struck bivouacs, and made ready to move forward through the fringe of broken hills, and thence on to the plain. We were to attack El Haud exactly as we had done previously. Stealthily advancing in artillery formation we crossed the plain, and at a certain point opened out in extended order. Long before reaching the foothills the enemy had discovered our approach, and a line of bright flashes warned us that they were not to be taken by surprise this time. As we got nearer the bullets began to find their victims. Here and there men were hit, some falling in a crumpled heap to cry out for the last time, others writhing in the agony of their wounds; whilst those whose hurts were but slight, hastily bandaged themselves with their " field-dressing," and rendered what succour they could to their less fortunate comrades. But the advancing lines passed on into the darkness, quicker and quicker as the incentive took hold of each man to hurry on to the foothills and get some sort of cover. What mattered if the Turks were there? It would be a straight fight. The flashes broke out afresh accompanied by the monotonous knocking sound of the machine guns. Stepping reverently over a dead form here, and closing up a gap there, each man trusted to God to see him through. When you are face to face with death like this peculiar thoughts flash through your mind, and you realize that each one of them may be your last.

At dawn the hills were reached, and by a tremendous effort we captured the enemy's first line of defence and gained a footing on them, but only a footing, and at heavy cost. All the higher positions dominating our own were strongly occupied by the enemy, of whom there appeared to be thousands. By some unknown means they had dragged mountain and small field guns up there, with which they fired at us continually, while every hill-top and ridge seemed to bristle with machine guns.

It was fatal to expose yourself, for as sure as you did a bullet would come whizzing past your ear, or perhaps would not pass at all.

The Battalion on our right had come to a stand-still, so having got so far, it was impossible for us to get farther without exposing our flank. Every piece of cover was used to its fullest advantage, and we simply had to lie still and await developments.

All that morning a continual procession of wounded men made their way back to the dressing station, some light hearted in spite of their wounds, others trying to be; some limping along unaided and making good progress, others lying painfully upon stretchers, their faces pale, and their bodies a mass of bloody bandages.

Meanwhile, the mounted troops had penetrated through the hills to the north, and by sun-down had captured Es Salt, leaving one Brigade to guard the left flank. On the following day, May 1st, this force was obliged to retire, being attacked by enemy cavalry and infantry who had crossed the Jordan higher up. A combined attack was then arranged between the cavalry against Es Salt from the east, and our Brigade from the west, in an endeavour to surround and capture the enemy force at Shunet Nimrin.

Again we tried to advance, but our endeavours were useless. In one instance two platoons had to cross a ridge and advance up the wady on the opposite side. They reached the ridge, but as soon as they attempted to proceed farther a murderous fire was opened upon them. Those who were left of the right platoon, only half of the original number, succeeded in reaching the bottom where they were comparatively safe, but the other platoon was confronted by a precipice down which it was impossible to climb, and they were caught there in the fire from the enemy positions towering above them. The officer and sergeant and several men were killed outright. Some of the survivors made for a small cave where they thought they would be safe, but it proved a death-trap. The Turks simply fired into the mouth of the cave, and one by one these poor fellows were killed. By this time only a Lance-Corporal and nine men remained of a platoon of about thirty, and their plight seemed hopeless. The Corporal asked for a volunteer to take a report back to Company Headquarters. It was a job attended by the utmost danger, for no sooner did a man move from his little bit of cover than sure

enough he attracted fire from the ever-watchful Turks.
Although it meant running the gauntlet with but a
faint hope of getting through alive, one man, Private
Cruickshank (the same who had such a marvellous
escape on El Muntar) offered to take that chance.
Both sides of the ridge were exposed to the enemy,
but Cruickshank chose that down which the remnants
of the other platoon had gone earlier.   As soon as he
moved he was greeted with a shower of bullets, one
hitting him in the arm.   With as much haste as the
rocky nature of the ground would permit he began the
descent, but fell wounded in the thigh.   Getting up
again, undaunted, he hobbled on but fell an easy
target to that merciless fire, and with some half-dozen
more bullet wounds in his leg he lay for a few seconds
panting.   It would have been fatal to have lain there
long, so realizing this he began to roll.   Over and
over he went, bumping against stones and boulders,
but never stopping until he reached the bottom.   All
the while the Turks in their determination to destroy
him, kept up a hot fire, but he was mercifully saved
from further wounds.   By a piece of amazing good
fortune he alighted among several men belonging to
the other platoon, all wounded, who were sheltering
behind a large rock.   By dint of much squeezing
together into one corner they made room for him, and
there they remained all the day until at night a party
of stretcher-bearers came along and carried them
back to safety.   For his gallantry and self-sacrifice
Cruickshank won the Victoria Cross, this being the
second awarded in our Battalion.

That night, as many bodies as could be found in
the dark were brought in and laid together in readiness.
Two wagons arrived from our Headquarters.   They
were empty.   We all knew what was their mission,

but as though we needed telling, one of the drivers coolly remarked that he had "come for the stiffs." Oh, why do some men stoop to profanity on occasions which demand their deepest reverence and sympathy? They have *no* respect for death or for those whom it has claimed; they are usually men who have never been face to face with death or danger.

Each lifeless body was lifted into the wagons; ten, twenty, thirty and more, the very best of fellows; men with whom we had lived, with whom we had laughed, men with whom we had discussed the past and planned the future, now all covered with blood and dust, tattered and disfigured—dead. It was a horrible sight.

As each corpse was lifted up, we half expected to hear the old familiar laugh or the same cheerful voice. There had been no last look, no parting words. Not a sound broke the grim silence save the dull thud as each limp form found its place at the bottom of the wagon. When all were in, the wagons rumbled away with their ghastly loads.

Upon a sandy knoll, surrounded by small trees and bushes, about two thousand yards east of the Jordan, a quiet and peaceful spot, is a little cemetery of between thirty and forty graves. In them lie as many gallant Crusaders who have added their names to the vast roll of those who, before them, have similarly given their lives for the same great cause. Our Battalion, just over two hundred strong, was relieved, and under cover of night withdrew to the broken ground on the eastern bank of the river. The following evening, just as the light was fading, we left camp and repaired to the little cemetery. Forming a hollow square round the rows of open graves, we stood with heads bared, bowed over reversed rifles.

Q

The Padre read the Burial Service, and the pipers wailed a coronach. Never did music sound so sweet in our ears, nor yet so plaintive. The last notes of the bagpipes died away, and all was still; not a murmur as, for a few seconds, we paid silent homage to our dead comrades. A firing party stepped forward, there was a rattling of bolts, a whispered order, and one after the other three volleys rent the air.

We marched back to our bivouacs a very silent body of men. The ceremony was too impressive and the occasion too solemn to be consigned to the labyrinths of the memory unhallowed by a fitting period of silence.

.   .   .   .

The mounted force at Es Salt was attacked by enemy troops from Amman, which prevented them from assisting in the attack on Shunet Nimrin from the north-east. The promised assistance from the Arabs failed to materialize, more enemy reinforcements were reported to be on their way from the north, and as we were unable to make progress from the west and so drive the Turks back into the hands of the cavalry, a withdrawal was ordered. The retirement of the mounted troops was a very hazardous undertaking accomplished only with the greatest difficulty.

Concentrating amongst the scrub from whence we had first set out upon the ill-fated expedition, we snatched an hour or two of sleep, and just before dawn recrossed the river by the suspension bridge, a sorrowful and broken Battalion, reduced by half. But, as we marched mournfully back to Jericho, we were not unmindful of the other half of the Battalion nor the mercies by which we had been spared.

CHAPTER XXII

CONCLUSION

An air of sadness reigned over our little camp amongst the Spina Christi near Jericho—an atmosphere of leaden depression. Strive as we would it could not be dispelled; the dusky curtains of sorrow were gathered around, but the gloom hid nothing from the eyes of the mind. Turn in what direction we would we were faced with a dozen reminders of our grief, the absent bivouac companions, the gloomy silence, the downcast expression of those who had been spared where so many had fallen. Let it not be said that we were ultra-sentimental! If there be any who have never known the blank that follows death—the dreary void to which the strongest mind cannot remain insensible—when something familiar and inseparable from your everyday life is missed at every turn, when a cheery voice or friendly banter which has been part of your existence, and from time to time has helped to pass many a weary hour, no longer greets you—if there be any who have not known this, then they can never faintly understand the effect our great loss had upon us.

We stayed at Jericho two days. In the evening of the second day we started on our way back to Jerusalem once more. We were conveyed in motor lorries—an unprecedented piece of good fortune for

243

us, which rather seemed like a mark of thanks on the part of the powers-that-be for our services. It was by no means a comfortable journey, but then, we did not look for comfort. For my own part, I was in an agony of both body and mind. I ached in every limb and my back seemed as though it would break. Although the atmosphere of the plain was warm and heavy I shook like a leaf. The symptoms were too well known for there to be any doubt as to their cause; those pestilential mosquitoes had done their work and I was in the firm grip of our other enemy—Malaria.

Before we reached the Mount of Olives heavy rain began to fall. By the time we got to our old camping ground at Shafat everything was saturated, but we put up our bivouacs and made the best of it.

The next morning the Colonel required a map of El Haud to be drawn from memory and, if you please, showing contours. The object of this map was to show how preponderatingly superior the enemy's positions had been to our own, which were overlooked on all sides. General Shea was coming that afternoon to address the Battalion and, presumably, a conference was to be held on the recent operations.[1] I finished the map; fortunately the shakiness of the lines was lost in the intricacies of the contours and rather assisted in demonstrating the point involved.

.   .   .   .

The scene was a bell tent in the vast Base Depot at Kantara; the time about 8 p.m. on November 11th, 1918. Through the thick haze of tobacco smoke

[1] The second crossing of the Jordan was the last engagement of the Second Battalion "London Scottish" in Palestine before returning to France.

two candles could be seen battling for existence, disclosing a little group of men quietly playing at cards. Behind them were two chess enthusiasts deeply engrossed in a knotty problem.

A few days previously news had been received of General Allenby's magnificent cavalry drive to Damascus, the resulting debacle of the Turkish Army giving rise to many and various conjectures as to the likely sequel.

On peering into the tent to watch these men, all intent upon their game, it would have been difficult to imagine that anything unusual was in the air. But that something extraordinary was about to happen, or had actually happened, was certain from the sudden arrival of a man very much out of breath with the haste he had made, and evidently bursting with news to tell. He rushed into the tent, caught his foot in some equipment, and sprawled headlong over the cards and players, raising a torrent of remonstration.

" Armistice signed," he spluttered, after he had spat out a mouthful of sand.

But these hardened campaigners had heard this before. They had even been told to expect the " cease hostilities " signal in the form of blue Very Lights when wallowing in the mud of France in 1916.

" Don't you hear? Armistice has been signed," the new-comer repeated with emphasis.

" I didn't know they had any beer in the canteen," caustically remarked one of the players as he collected the scattered cards.

" You're ten years too soon," said one of the chess enthusiasts, looking up from the board.

The bearer of the best news they had heard for years glanced from one to another with an injured look upon his face, and becoming exasperated at the incredulity displayed, went to great pains in relating how, as he was passing the camp notice-board five minutes before, he had seen a large crowd clamouring round it striking matches in order to read a news telegram. He had not been able to get near enough to read the news himself, but had learned that an Armistice had been signed and hostilities had ceased.

At that moment another man arrived, also suffering considerably from loss of breath, who corroborated the intelligence that official news had really come through of an Armistice in all the theatres of war.

" Well, I'm blowed," said one of the amazed listeners.

" At last," softly murmured another, with a sigh which spoke volumes.

"And quite time too," rejoined a third, giving it as his firm opinion that it was high time mankind stopped fighting and destroying, and settled down to decent civilized life again, employing itself upon some useful occupation for the betterment of the world generally.

" Hand round the doings, Jim," said the idealist, and the cards were dealt again, pipes and cigarettes were lit, and the chess board set to rights after the disturbance; no hilarity, no wild manifestation, no idiotic excesses.

A few rockets were sent up from the neighbouring aerodrome and the men across at the railway set fog signals on a length of line and ran a locomotive over them; but that was all. The troops to whom this glad news meant so much, received it quietly and soberly. All were deeply immersed in their own thoughts, and if we but knew, their hearts were lifted up that night in thankfulness to God for bringing to an end the horrible bloodshed, suffering and destruction that had ravaged the world for four weary years.

INDEX

*Printed for Messrs. H. F. & G. Witherby by
Northumberland Press Limited, Newcastle-on-Tyne*

4379516R00155

Printed in Great Britain
by Amazon.co.uk, Ltd.,
Marston Gate.